Let it Out

Let it Out

a journey through journaling

KATIE DALEBOUT

HAY HOUSE, INC.

Carlsbad, California • New York City
London • Sydney • Johannesburg
Vancouver • New Delhi

Published and distributed in the United States by: Hay House, Inc.: www.hayhouse
.com® • *Published and distributed in Australia by:* Hay House Australia Pty. Ltd.: www
.hayhouse.com.au • *Published and distributed in the United Kingdom by:* Hay House UK,
Ltd.: www.hayhouse.co.uk • *Published and distributed in the Republic of South Africa by:*
Hay House SA (Pty), Ltd.: www.hayhouse.co.za • *Distributed in Canada by:* Raincoast
Books: www.raincoast.com • *Published in India by:* Hay House Publishers India: www
.hayhouse.co.in

Cover design: Laura Evangelista • *Interior design:* Pamela Homan

Library of Congress Cataloging-in-Publication Data

Names: Dalebout, Katie, date.
Title: Let it out : a journey through journaling / Katie Dalebout.
Description: Carlsbad, California : Hay House, Inc., 2016.
Identifiers: LCCN 2015037284 | ISBN 9781401947446 (paperback)
Subjects: LCSH: Diaries--Authorship. | Diaries--Therapeutic use. |
  Self-actualization (Psychology)
Classification: LCC PN4390 .D36 2016 | DDC 808.06/692--dc23 LC record available at
http://lccn.loc.gov/2015037284

Tradepaper ISBN: 978-1-4019-4744-6

10 9 8 7 6 5
1st edition, April 2016

SUSTAINABLE
FORESTRY
INITIATIVE
Certified Chain of Custody
Promoting Sustainable Forestry
www.sfiprogram.org
SFI-01268
SFI label applies to the text stock

Printed in the United States of America

To my podcast
listeners: I wrote this
for you. Actually I wrote it
for me, and then realized it would
probably help you if it helped me.
It wouldn't exist without you.
You gave me a reason to
authentically share myself and
learn right along with you.
Thank you. This is for you.

CONTENTS

FOREWORD

Since my teen years, I've had a journal by my bedside. It's been my guide through heartache, addiction recovery, life transitions, and miraculous shifts. Most important, I've used the practice of journaling to receive inspiration and channel guidance far beyond my physical sight.

A journal is a companion that will always be there to listen, receive, and hold space for whatever you need to release. Creating a relationship with your journal can guide you toward great spiritual connection and a sense of intimacy unlike any other. Journaling is a sacred process.

I'm not alone in my love affair with journaling. My dear friend Katie Dalebout is a journaling cheerleader. Her enthusiasm for the practice has guided her to heal her fear-based perceptions of herself and step into her authentic power. As Katie says in the Introduction to this book, "Journaling saved me. It was the door to my spiritual path." Through her personal transformation she has been called to teach others how to do the same. In this book Katie offers you life-changing practices that you can use to make your journal your companion on your transformational journey inward.

Katie is a true Spirit Junkie. Her commitment to her personal growth and her miracle mind-set are immeasurable. It has been a privilege to witness her path and see her step into her power as a leader and teacher. Katie is a powerful example for anyone ready to clear the blocks to the presence of their purpose and light.

Apply the practices in this book to any area of your life that needs a shift. Trust in the process, and know that each time you surrender your inner wisdom to the page you will experience a miracle.

Let Katie be your guide as you let out anything holding you back to create space for manifesting your new vision.

— *Gabrielle Bernstein*

INTRODUCTION

My Journey into Journaling

You want change. You've heard about affirmations, but aren't totally sure if they work. You like the concept of positive thinking, but haven't noticed any differences in your life. Maybe you like yoga, but you take off before *savasana;* or maybe you've attempted meditating, but your mind is a circus. Whether you've read the entire self-help section of the bookstore in vain or wouldn't be caught dead in that area of Barnes & Noble, you crave change.

Perhaps your career isn't what you thought it would be, but you feel stuck on how to fix your situation. Maybe your relationships aren't what you thought they would be, but you're unsure how to shift or repair them. Perhaps your location isn't where you thought you'd end up, but money's tight, and making a move doesn't seem possible. Maybe you have a grand vision for your life—dreams of moving to New York City and being welcomed like you were Taylor Swift, creating your dream job, and being in a loving, committed relationship—but you aren't clear on the smallest steps that need to happen to get you there.

The *real* reason you haven't achieved your vision for the life you desire? Deep down, you might not believe that you

1

deserve it . . . or that it's even possible for you. You might not even be sure where to begin. You wish someone would hold your hand and tell you exactly what to do, coach you through it. And not just anyone—a friend with a fresh and loving voice who has actually been there and created lasting change in her own life.

That's me. I'm your girl. Hi.

I used to be in the same place of wanting change, feeling stuck, and hitting wall after wall—and journaling saved me. It was the door to my spiritual path; it helped me get clear on the feelings and thoughts that were swirling around in my head. Writing was the only way for me to not only discover what those thoughts were—but to *let them out* and start to build the life I wanted. My journal was my greatest tool in finding my purpose, healing myself, and getting started on my life's path.

Usually, it's the same few thoughts stuck on repeat that get caught in our minds, and thus keep *us* stuck. Journaling is the plumber that can unclog the mind (that's bogged down with *years* of old gunk) and clear out repetitive, destructive thoughts and beliefs. By letting out your thoughts, you become objective—you become an observer of your life, and with clarity you step into a position of power to choose how *you* want to run the show and guide your life.

If you feel you've tried everything—or if you have no idea even where to begin—then this book is the missing puzzle piece that can take your life to the next level by creating lasting change through the practice of journaling. The tools offered in here are powerful yet simple activities that can be done *anywhere* and *in any order*. They're the tools that have transformed my life and the lives of many of my clients. And when I say above that journaling saved me, I don't mean that as a figure of speech. It quite literally rescued me from my own mind . . .

The Mean Girls in My Mind

Before I discovered journaling, from an outside perspective my life seemed fine, with all the trappings of young success: a loving, supportive family; a college education; a promising full-time job right out of college with a clear career path—everything we've always assumed to bring happiness and success.

Or so it seemed.

Internally, loud and fearful thoughts clouded my mind: *You're going to be stuck in this job forever and never live your dreams. Moving is impossible for you; you don't have enough money. You're a fraud and nobody reads your blog anyways. Why do you even have a blog? Why did you eat that? You're disgusting. You've always been the ugly girl and always will. You should just give up now while it seems like you have it together.* Yes, my thoughts were an inner mean girl that would put Regina George to shame. I would never say the terrible, negative things I said to myself to a friend or even out loud—but in my head I had free range to beat myself to a pulp, which I did on the regular.

My favorite author, Elizabeth Gilbert, often refers to her mind as a neighborhood you wouldn't want to wander in alone at night. I related to that line immensely and felt embarrassed about the inner workings of my mind, which were flooded with shame and negativity. As a child, teen, and young adult, these scattered thoughts plagued my life—but in ways that weren't apparent to anyone but me.

As I look back now, the reason I was deemed a "Chatty Cathy" as a child, "accident-prone" as a teen, and "scattered" as a young woman was because I wasn't making sense of what was up in my mind. There were so many thoughts telling me *I'm not good enough* or *I'm not deserving* that they deeply buried the kind and gentle part of me under the weight of self-cruelty.

I wasn't addressing the negative thoughts I had about my body, which led to the insecurities I had about my life in general, and how I felt so alone even though I was surrounded by people; instead, I was quieting them by absorbing myself in TV, socializing with friends, and working hard in school. I wasn't talking about these thoughts, either. I was doing everything *except* really feeling my deep-down emotions and insecurities. I wasn't ready to get to know myself and sort through my deep-rooted insecurities, find out where they came from, and learn how I could release them for good. It seemed easier to zone out in all the normal socially accepted ways than face my thoughts, emotions, and severe lack of self-confidence.

This changed when I realized my thoughts had power. Ironically, I learned the power of my mind through my body hitting rock bottom.

Judging My Worth in Weight

I hated my body. This started in elementary school. There was never a comment or a look that spurred my feeling this way; I just felt different, and believed my fate was to hate my body. Shopping for first communion dresses cemented this when I needed a size 10 and heard all my friends still fit in size 8s. From there I was constantly comparing my size with other kids'; I would judge my worth based on my weight. Each year, my fear of gaining weight made me play small—and this fear was consuming. On any given morning in high school, I might feel completely fine, and then one ill-fitting pair of jeans or an unflattering photo surfacing on Facebook would completely take me out, leading me to vigilantly control my food and obsess about any exercise I could do to change. I kept spiraling into a consuming body hate.

With my tiny confidence and huge fear, by the end of college (where I had the autonomy to successfully control my food), I was in the midst of a full-blown eating disorder, which eventually brought me to my knees, as everyone around me realized what was going on. I was called into a meeting with my professors and told I couldn't finish my senior semester unless I sought medical help; I was confronted by my yoga teachers and told that I couldn't practice hot yoga anymore because they were afraid my heart would stop while I was in class; I spent hours crying and arguing with my concerned family—all the while telling everyone I was fine.

I wasn't fine. But it wasn't just my body that was deprived; it wasn't that simple. It was my thoughts that were lacking love. I was so mean to myself that I knew addressing my thoughts had to come before I could make any lasting physical changes. I felt like no one understood that until I met a coach who got what I was going through because she'd been through it herself. My coach led me to spirituality, meditation, and the teachings of Gabby Bernstein, who taught me to heal my physical body through healing my mind. It was a crazy concept to me at the time: meditation and positive thinking as a way to heal my low weight and shutting-down organs? But I was scared and desperate—the perfect combination to be hyper-receptive to a radical method. As I found out, our lowest points are often the catalysts for our deepest change.

I attempted meditating, and even forced it by going to classes and workshops in unfamiliar wellness centers that smelled of patchouli and where I was regularly the only student. Desperate for relief—and knowing that my coach was on to something with mindfulness—I pushed hard to force meditation to "work." Let me say, discipline has never been an issue for me. I could be disciplined enough to stick to a certain diet (even when obsessive and restrictive), and I could be disciplined enough to follow an exercise routine, so when it came to sitting in stillness both morning and evening to meditate, no problem—I could do that, too. Pop in my headphones and I was good to go.

However, I was just going through the motions to check off daily meditation on my to-do list. I was meditating out of necessity and fear and obligation. And fear as my motivation could only get me so far.

My motivation to eat "healthy" was based in fear as well: a fear of becoming overweight. But this wasn't what I was really afraid of. My real fear was what I believed being overweight would *mean*. I attached *thinness* to *confidence, beauty,* and *happiness*; and I attached *fat* to *being alone, unworthy,* and *doomed*. I couldn't see that my weight had nothing to do with my self-worth, and that I could be confident, beautiful, and happy at any size. I was too stuck in my fear story to see outside of it. It was only after years of therapy, coaching, and the work of emotional-eating expert Isabel Foxen Duke that I recognized that my fear, though it seemed so strong and real at the time, was false. It was only stemming from crazy perceptions I'd picked up from society, which skewed the way I viewed reality.

I realized that my deep-rooted fear of being alone, unworthy, and doomed motivated me right into my eating disorder. Once I understood this, I could clearly see that my motivation *couldn't* be fear if I wanted real change.

So love became my motivation. And that's when the real shift happened.

Control Is Overrated

I learned that loving my body as it was was what I needed to do. I only had to focus on each present moment, and not worry if my body was going to change. I had to start to treat my body with love and as my ally, not an enemy. If I wanted to practice yoga, heal my relationships, and have a full life, I had to truly take care of myself—not just *pretend* to be "healthy" as my mask for trying to stay super thin.

I shifted my motivation for healthy eating toward love. My passion for life was more important than my fear. I wanted to eat healthfully most of the time for vitality—to climb mountains, teach yoga, speak, blog, write, and fall in love—and not just to manipulate my body to look a certain way. I also realized the importance of pleasure and enjoyment of food and trusting that no matter what I chose to eat, if the decision was made from a place of genuine love rather than fear, all was well. It didn't matter then *what* I ate as much as how I felt about what I ate.

Eventually I recognized that I had grasped tightly for control of my body because I felt I couldn't control my life. The truth is, we *don't* actually have control of everything in life, and surrendering to that truth is a catalyst to true happiness. When we realize we're not in control, we can sit back, relax, and enjoy the unfolding of what is, instead of holding on tightly and trying to manage every detail of our existence.

We all cope in different ways to avoid feeling the uncertainty of life, whether it be through food or addictions or any number of outlets. Releasing control and trusting our destiny takes practice, which I desperately needed. I was drawn to meditation and spirituality as a way to bring me into the present moment—the only moment we have any control over—and let go of the future, which is out of our hands. If you believe, like I do, that your thoughts inform your reality, then in a way you *can* influence your future—but only through your thoughts in the present.

The level of emotional and physical health I craved could only be reached by letting go of control. Meditating seemed like a perfect solution to bring myself into the present by focusing on my breath, but I just couldn't do it. My thoughts were too loud. Something was missing.

After months of relentless meditating, I finally put my finger on it. How could I clear my mind of thoughts, or even focus on a single idea or mantra, when I didn't even know what all the thoughts in my mind *were*? I wasn't allowing myself to define them, feel them, or figure out where they came from. I would sit with my thoughts passing by, sometimes for hours, but how could I finally *let them out*?

The answer came in one word: *journaling.*

Say Hello to My New Best Friend

My journal became my best friend, my boyfriend, my doctor, and my coach. I'd write to myself, to my parents, to my coach, and even to God/Mother Earth/the Universe/Source (whatever you want to call it). I wrote down all the things I was thinking but never saying. I would, in the words of my mentor, author, and coach Nancy Levin, "admit to myself what I already knew to be true." By putting these deep thoughts and fears down on paper, I acknowledged their presence—and was one step closer to releasing them, along with each of my failed attempts at control.

My journaling techniques miraculously made my life come together in ways I never imagined. I discovered that meditating was impossible for me without first releasing the thoughts that were playing on repeat in my head. I couldn't quiet my circus-mind without first figuring out what was in there and acknowledging it by writing it out. I could get full sentences out of my intuition by journaling as opposed to meditation, since it was a dialogue with all the different voices in my mind.

Aware of what these practices were doing in my life, and wondering if I was the only human who would have this powerful experience with letting out her thoughts, I started coaching other girls on developing a journaling practice. Predictably, their results with my writing tools mirrored my own. That's when I knew I was on to something with this journaling thing and that these tools were undoubtedly powerful—and therefore must be shared.

Unlike meditation, the journaling process was easy and familiar to start. Writing came naturally for me because as a "talker," I had a lot to say, so I just wrote how I spoke. However, I realized writing didn't come that easy for everyone. And even though it did for me, looking back, I sure wish I'd had a guidebook to help me get deep into the places in my mind I didn't want to visit, and often didn't even know existed. So I decided to create exactly what I wanted: a book with all my useful journaling activities to be shared and experienced. I wanted everyone to have access to the tools, activities, and practices I learned that helped me feel better, find my voice, become more present, and ultimately define my purpose.

I ended up extensively researching my new obsession and found scientific proof of the hypothesis I had come to myself: Journaling has tremendous positive outcomes for those who practice it consistently, including improved health. In a 2001 study published in the *Journal of Experimental Psychology,* Professors Kitty Klein and Adriel Boals of North Carolina State University concluded that there are indeed beneficial effects of expressive writing, particularly when used to express deep or stressful thoughts and feelings. Such writing was shown to lead to fewer doctor visits, improved immune function, increased antibody production, and greater mental well-being—continuing even months after the experiment.

The Most Nonjudgmental Friend You Could Ever Have

Maybe you're thinking that this is all well and good, but you hate writing. Perhaps journaling is a painful process for you, or you fear that nothing will come out of you. No worries—I got you; that's why this book exists. People give me that smack about resistance to writing when I even mention the practice of journaling, and although I love writing now, I can relate. I hated long writing assignments in school. I'm no Elizabeth Gilbert or Jane Austen, but I write as medicine. Think of this book and these tools as a prescription to feel better and, to quote the Nike slogan, "just do it," and the results will keep you going. I will guide you step-by-step with questions that get into the corners of your mind and prompts that nudge you to explore untapped areas.

If you're still uncertain, think of it this way: When someone wants to start eating more healthfully, they don't begin by gnawing away at raw kale. Rather, they learn clever ways to incorporate kale so it's digestible, doable, and even pleasurable. They may add a tiny bit into a soup or a fruit smoothie. Similarly, I take this new, powerful superfood of a practice—journaling—and make it digestible and pleasurable so it becomes something you eventually crave.

Whether you're an experienced novelist or you failed high school English, this type of writing *is* innate to you. If you can speak, you can write. There's no grade and no way to fail, other than by not trying it at all. Just write like you speak. In this modern time, we all write daily. If you can write a text message or a tweet or an e-mail, you can journal. Journaling is basically texting your feelings to the most nonjudgmental friend you could ever have.

I've worked with many life coaches and coached many people myself, and these tools are essentially self-coaching techniques to examine your thoughts. We have over 60,000 thoughts a day, most of which are repeated thoughts we also had yesterday and will have tomorrow. What journaling, and particularly this book, helps you do is become aware of what your brain is thinking on autopilot, while asking you great questions that will lead you to great answers to life's perplexities.

This is not a book where I tell you the answers to questions about your life, because I don't have them; the answers are within *you.* I will, however, guide you to claim them—or rather, let them out with prompts and inquiries to locate your answers. At first the process might seem challenging and your thoughts might be alarming, especially if you haven't examined them before. They might be disturbingly negative, like the inner mean girl that plagued me. But even if so, keep going—eventually your thoughts can change, but you have to first become *aware* of them. And once your thoughts change, your life can change, too. What you think informs how you feel, and how you feel leads to what actions you take, which leads to creating success in your life. This isn't a onetime life fix; rather, the goal is that journaling becomes a lifelong habit, helping you navigate your constantly changing thoughts, which create your spectrum of emotions, which creates your actions and therefore the results of your life.

Why Do We Need This Extra Step in Working with Our Minds?

Modern psychotherapist Ashley Turner teaches that our inner voices are like a board of directors. We have the director of finance, the inner parent, and the inner child, among many others. Journaling allows you to see which of those voices tends to run the show while the other ones are quiet. You'll also see that just because one voice says something, that doesn't mean it's true. Letting it out on paper allows you to filter out beliefs that you don't want to hold on to any longer.

Journaling allows you to stop identifying with your negative beliefs or thought patterns and instead see yourself as separate from them. You start to move from judging yourself to simply witnessing your thoughts, cozying up with them, learning from them, and ultimately letting them out.

Once you release the negative smoke clouding your mind, you can allow in more and more positive thoughts, which will create more and more positive feelings and then positive experiences. I'm a student of Abraham-Hicks and believe our thoughts create our reality. Meaning, if we're focused on worry, negativity, and fear, that's what we'll experience. Likewise, if we focus on excitement, positivity, and love, *that's* what we'll experience. Journaling is the tool to help you truly make that shift, since simply slapping some positivity on a plate full of negative won't make the meal suddenly happy.

The processes in this book allow you to first examine, experience, and digest whatever is already on your plate before adding in anything new, regardless of how delicious those things are. I'll guide you to figure out what you want to add as well as what you need to remove to create space for the new.

And you guys—journaling rocks! I'm so psyched and passionate to share that because it's worked for me in some pretty radical ways (more on that below). Journaling, however, is a process, and the techniques I share will guide you through every bit of it—tool by tool, step-by-step, and section by section, with me holding your hand the entire way. This book will be your companion in all your crucial moments whenever you reach for it. It will be there through whatever you need to *let out*.

Being Nudged by Inspiration

Before I get you going on the interactive portion of this book, I want to tell you a story of how I witnessed my own power with these tools. Cool? So sit back, relax, and allow me to tell you one of my favorite examples of using these high-vibe techniques in manifesting something I really wanted in my life. Don't get too comfortable here, though, because for the majority of this book you'll be the one doing the writing—not me! I'm just here to gently nudge you in the divine direction to see your blind spots and shift into the manifesting powers that are available to us all. Following that intuitive nudging can take you to super groovy places.

In fact, that nudging is why this book even came into fruition.

Creating a book had been a dream of mine in college. I fantasized about being a published author and having my words in print help people through sharing my own experience. As an avid consumer of self-help, spirituality, and personal development, I admired the work of authors like Louise Hay, Gabrielle Bernstein, Kris Carr, and Nancy Levin.

When I realized writing a book was actually possible—it turned from a dream into an inspired knowing, which was revealed to me one morning in a journaling session I'll never forget—I was so excited and lit up by my literary aspirations that I told everyone I knew. But everyone I told responded with reasons why I *couldn't* publish a book:

"You're just a kid."

"Writing a book requires experience."

"You'd be a first-time author and therefore you'd need an agent, an expense you don't have the funds for."

"You need to focus on a full-time job to support yourself."

"You need a fan base of over 30,000 people, at least."

"Write an e-book—no one is publishing books these days."

And so on. The list of reasons I received for why I couldn't write a book could have been a book *itself*—a book I chose not to read. My energy was focused elsewhere.

At that point, I was a devoted student of spirituality and the principles my fellow Hay House authors teach, including the Law of Attraction and positive psychology, so I knew to not allow any of those negative influences penetrate me and kill my dream. Rather, I remained on the path of knowing: I knew so deeply in my bones that I would someday have my book published with my dream publishing house. I didn't have an agent, a degree in writing, or years of experience, but I did have a dream, and I just knew it would happen.

I stayed wide-open, hoping an opportunity would come to me . . . but nothing came. So I got that full-time job with benefits and the 401(k) that my mom encouraged, but I remained steadfast that my dream would still eventually materialize. I had no clue how, but I didn't get wrapped up in trying to control that; instead, I focused on the end result rather than the plan. Teacher and author Mike Dooley says that the "cursed hows" keep people stuck—so I focused exclusively on the end result, knowing that the "how" wasn't my concern and would someday find *me.*

The Radio Ad That Changed My Life

One day at work I was listening to Hay House Radio and heard a commercial for their Writer's Workshop event in New York City. I lived in Detroit, and so the distance was relatively close; my ears perked up and I turned up the volume. What I heard next gave me full-body chills: The workshop was led by three keynote speakers who just happened to be my top three favorite authors: Gabrielle Bernstein, Kris Carr, and Nancy Levin. My stomach dropped as if I were on a huge roller coaster. I knew I had to be there. Guys, I can't even explain to you the feeling—no, it was a deep knowing—that I *had* to be there.

I listened more and heard that the workshop was also a contest. At the conference, the CEO of Hay House, Reid Tracy, would teach about the publishing industry and how to write a successful book proposal. Participants would then have the opportunity to write a proposal and submit it for the chance to win a publishing deal with Hay House. I leapt up from my desk, called my mom, and explained that I finally had a request for a birthday present this year, after years of never giving her a wish list. This year for my 22nd (my lucky number) birthday, I knew what I wanted more than anything on earth: to go to this conference.

I remember ending the conversation like this: "Mom, I know I can win this contest; trust me." As the words came out of me, I listened to them as if I were listening to someone else saying them, and I thought, *Pardon? How the hell do you know that? You don't even have a topic for a book, you suck at spelling, and writing is hard work.* I pushed those negative thoughts away, jumped online, and booked a flight to New York for both my mother and me.

A few months later, there I was, sitting in the Hotel Pennsylvania listening to my mentors speak about how to write a book. I remember bawling during Kris Carr's moving lecture about writing her way through her journey from cancer patient to cancer thriver. I remember shaking the first time I met my mentor Gabby and having her call me out and ask me to stand up when she mentioned her target audience and how I was basically the girl she wrote her first book to, and years later here she was, signing it for me. I remember having full-body chills listening to Nancy Levin read her moving, raw, beautiful poetry and show me the power of writing.

I listened to every word, took copious notes, gave them hugs and thanked them for their books, and loved every minute of being there. I'll never forget that hot New York weekend and the fellow writers I ate lunch with each day, sweating on the stairs of Madison Square Garden, who have since become dear friends and my support system. The entire thing truly felt magical.

After the last day of the workshop, I sat across the table at Hu Kitchen with my mom, eating kale chips and gushing for hours about how amazing the conference was, all the best friends I'd just met, what it was like basically snuggling my mentors, and most of all how "this book proposal thing" was really hard.

And I remember it was there where I decided I wasn't going to participate in the contest and write a book proposal . . . although I didn't have the heart to tell my mom.

I couldn't admit this to her. She had just given up her weekend, missed my grandma's birthday party, spent the past few days wandering solo around scorching NYC while I was inside at the workshop, and listened to me gush every evening about how I would be an author someday—so no, telling her I wasn't even going to *attempt* to write the proposal wasn't an option. I had rationalized to myself that merely attending the workshop, getting photos with my gurus, and meeting new friends was enough to say we got our money's worth, and I considered the weekend a success. There was no reason I needed to actually follow through and submit a proposal to the contest. After all, when was I going to have time to write it? I had a full-time job that required me to work events most weekends; I ran a blog that I loved and hosted a podcast; and I taught yoga and mentored girls in eating disorder recovery. To then take so much time to write a book proposal (one that would be judged against hundreds of other applicants, many of whom were much more experienced than me) was out of the question.

I will never forget when I finally decided to tell my mom about my decision to not submit a proposal. It was late October. I walked into my mom's house, home for a visit, and announced to her timidly, "Mom, I'm not going to write a book proposal for that contest we went to in June." I'd completely given up on my dream.

My mom, supportive of my decision, said, "Good, honey. Focus on your full-time job; you don't want to burn yourself out." In many ways she was right. Getting the proposal done could have burned me out, and I believe our parents, who love us infinitely, want us to be safe even above being happy sometimes. Focusing on my full-time work was definitely the safer choice.

Struck by Inspiration Lightning

The months passed, and I concentrated on my podcast, my blog, and most of all, my marketing job. I tried to put the January deadline of the contest out of my mind—but I kept thinking about it. I couldn't shake it. It would show up in my dreams, friends would ask me about it, and as much as I tried to forget it, it hung over my head like looming, unfinished homework.

Christmas came and went. Then one morning after New Year's, after journaling and sitting in a Kundalini meditation, I was struck. It felt like a jolt of lightning, like someone struck me with an idea—no, a mission that I had to take. I was inspired to write a book on journaling, the practice that had healed me.

That morning I just began writing; for hours my pen flowed on the page, never lifting off my bright-yellow legal pad. I was so inspired and in the flow that I let *Let It Out* pour out of me, word by word, until I had filled up the entire pad I was writing in. The only way I can describe it is that it felt like I was on an escalator: I just had to move a little bit, because regardless of how much I tried, *it* was moving *me* forward.

It all passed through me so quickly. I was flabbergasted yet simultaneously terrified.

The submission deadline was now just a week away, and I was nervous. Putting together a book proposal is a methodical process with specific requirements, including a competitive analysis and a promotional strategy—all of which I had no expertise with or time to complete. Even though the creative idea for the book passed through me very quickly, the actual construction of the proposal was more analytical, and I was positive it would be impossible to complete in less than a week.

At this point, though, I had no choice. Failing to submit the proposal was 10 billion times more painful than submitting but failing to win; not trying at all would be far too excruciating. So there I was, spending my evenings after insanely busy workdays desperately trying to figure out how to turn my morning journaling spew into a concrete book proposal to submit to my dream publisher. With the deadline imminent, time was of the essence, but like for most humans, procrastination is a tendency of mine.

Every time I'd try to work on it, I'd tell myself, *The time is not right*, or *I'm not inspired right now.* But something within me pushed me forward, word by word, line by line. The proposal got written in the early mornings that cold January, from 5 A.M. to 9 A.M., before I left for my full-time job for the day. Every time I wanted to stop, or was too burned out to keep going, or wanted to sleep in, I would use this mantra: *I got this.*

That line got me through, and that line got you this book.

Finally, and all too soon, it was the day the proposals were due, and I had mine just over half completed. I had come too far and worked too hard on it to completely give up, but the clock was ticking and I didn't have the day off from work to spend on it. I decided to keep trying. I worked for hours before work, took a lunch break to write, and then returned to it the second I got home. I had until midnight that night to complete it, so I pressed on. I was close but still had many details to finish, including my bio and making sure the formatting matched the strict proposal requirements.

Eleven forty-five P.M. came, and I still had two sections to complete. I contemplated giving up completely and cursed myself for not starting sooner (so many times . . . man, I made things stressful for myself)—for not beginning my proposal the day after I returned home from New York or *at least* a month or two out from the deadline. I felt defeated; I was close and had come so far, but there was no way I could finish the required sections of the proposal in a mere 15 minutes. I needed at least a few more hours. *If only I could lengthen days and manifest hours,* I wished. I contemplated turning it in halfway completed, but had remembered the sheer volume of entries they'd be receiving and that if I didn't follow directions I'd be disqualified anyway, so what was the point? *You should just go to bed—this is silly. Why are you doing this to yourself?* was all I heard in my head. I solemnly got up from my kitchen table and started to stretch and wash up for bed.

And then I was struck again, just like when I was jolted with the idea for the book in the first place that morning a week earlier. I remembered that Hay House was based in California and that the deadline was midnight Pacific time—and it was only 11:45 Eastern time, giving me three extra hours to complete the final sections of the proposal! Apparently, with a desire this strong I *could* manifest time. *Whoa.* Full-body chills washed over me. There was something going on that was bigger than me, as if some force in this universe really did see my worth more than I did in that moment. It felt like something was moving the players in the game on my behalf, orchestrating things for my highest good. There's a quote attributed to Rumi that says, "Life is rigged in your favor," and in that moment it truly felt as though it was.

An immediate sense of relief ensued as I relaxed back into my chair at my kitchen table where I'd spent the majority of the past week, and I completed the proposal with ease, sending it in with minutes to spare. I felt an amazing sense of accomplishment for writing the proposal and was unattached to the outcome. I was merely thrilled I had tried. Now that it was submitted, I could relish the excitement of finding out the winner. Whatever happened, I now knew I could write a book proposal and therefore had a skill I could use throughout my career to make my dream of being an author come true.

Unattached to Success

There was more than a month before the winners would be announced, and during that time I hardly thought of the contest. I had completely let go of the outcome. While I was hopeful and eager to find out who won, I was more just generally interested and excited to see which one of my friends from that magical writing workshop in New York earned the publishing deal. I was unattached to the aftermath because I was truly proud of completing the proposal and would be happy to publish my work as an e-book and simply sell it on my site. I surrendered the contest to the Universe and thought of the situation as a win-win.

The day the announcement was made, I was working at a huge yoga event. I was busy handling logistics and talking with thousands of yogis in a professional football stadium, when my friend grabbed me and told me I should go look at my phone because she had just seen something announced on the Hay House Facebook page. Being in the huge sports arena with barely any signal, I wasn't able to get a connection through my phone to see the announcement—but I did have a text message from a friend saying she was so excited for me she was crying. As soon as I read her text, I knew she could see what I couldn't on Facebook—that I had manifested the dream I had desired for so long: a publishing deal with my dream publisher. I screamed, simultaneously thrilled and shocked, and hugged my friends and even strangers near me. I said in my mind the words of Penny Lane in *Almost Famous*: "It's all happening." Just thinking of the moment gives me chills. Damn it was good.

All the doubts and fears about being an author subsided: the thoughts that I had no business winning, that I waited until the last minute, that I lacked the years of life experience to write a self-help book, and that I had no qualifications. Out of hundreds, my proposal stuck out for some reason, and I was chosen. This was the final nudge from the Universe I needed—telling me I was worthy and deserving of self-approval—all things I had desperately tried to seek through unhealthily manipulating my body and weight. Not everyone needs a book deal at 22 to receive this, but in some way this book was meant to be part of my path of true healing. It legitimized my dreams when I felt like no one else did and gave me the confidence to believe in myself. Like the Wizard of Oz, Hay House showed my Dorothy that it was possible to go beyond the limitations of my black-and-white worldview in my small town in Michigan and bust into a Technicolor world where dreams come true and life feels like an enchanted wonderland where everything is possible—a world I knew existed but didn't believe I could be part of. Winning this contest was my ticket to living in this magical wonderland, and it all started with me saying yes to inspiration, one hit of it at a time.

I was humbled and ecstatic by the news and immediately called my mom and my boss, thanking them for their love and support.

Practicing nonattachment to the outcome, I would learn, was the special sauce to manifesting my dream. The day after I found out I won, I was interviewing my guru Gabrielle Bernstein for my podcast, *The Wellness Wonderland Radio*. The timing couldn't have been better; it was a perfect example of the saying "the better it gets, the better it gets," as I felt like I was on cloud nine with all these awesome things happening to me in one weekend.

When I got on the phone with Gabby for the interview, she immediately congratulated me on winning, and as I told her how unattached I had been to the outcome, her wise response deeply struck me. She said with certainty, "Well, that's why you won—because you were unattached and let it go." She was right, even though I didn't consciously realize I was doing it at the time.

Being able to practice nonattachment and make peace in every situation has been the most freeing practice, and it's the change in my life that's changed everything. What's more, the ability to *let it go* stems directly from the ability to *let it out.* I hope having read my story, you will see what is available to you when you are open to guidance and when you use this book's tools—and just see what comes out of your mind onto paper. There were so many times when I didn't feel like continuing on my journey, when writing was the last thing I wanted to do, but as soon as I put pen to paper, my mind started to clear, that noisy "board of directors" began to quiet, and a new mental space was awakened, one of infinite possibilities. This is all available to you, too.

Seriously, anything is possible—if you don't believe that after hearing this story, go back and reread it. There's no denying miracles can happen if you're open to them happening and you move in their direction.

So find a comfy chair, brew a hot cup of tea, open your journal, grab your pen, and prepare to let it all out.

You got this.

THE USER MANUAL

Your Quick-Start Guide to Letting It Out

While you could skip right to the meat of this book, the Journaling Tool Kit, that wouldn't be very nice. Have you ever tried to set up a piece of Ikea furniture without first reading the instructions? While it's possible, it's much more difficult, and your furniture might not be very sturdy long-term. Think of the process of letting it out like setting up Ikea furniture. *You* will be so much more efficient and effective long-term if you follow the instructions first. Enjoy this user manual as your starting point for setting yourself up for journaling success.

Unlike anything else out there, *Let It Out* is not a workbook; it is *not* something you'll just complete once and then move on. What you hold in your hands is a diverse collection of exercises that you can turn to at any time for solace and self-discovery. You can approach the journaling tools chronologically, one day at a time, or you can flip to whichever tool is relevant to you on a particular day. Or maybe you'll let the Universe decide what you most need to address on a certain day, and close your eyes and pick a random page. Each experience is unique. Even if you return to the same journaling tool again and again, the outcome will be different every time because *you're* different each time you sit down to write.

The Route

> *"The race is long and, in the end, it's only with yourself."*
> — MARY SCHMICH

Along my own journey through journaling, I've discovered some crucial pointers for getting the most out of your writing sessions. So without further ado, here are some tips for the route . . .

Tip 1: Get Curious

Approach journaling like a scavenger hunt and this book like a treasure map—one that will lead you to your innermost feelings. The journey ahead is thrilling, but it's also new territory since you're going into the great unknown. Slight curiosity is all you need to get going. Get inquisitive about what you'll find on the route, and don't rush the process. It's not about where you end up, although that's sure to be incredible; it's much more about what you discover along the way. Savor every feeling and emotion that comes through while you're writing. What you find will be different every day. These tools are ever changing because *you* are.

Tip 2: Dance with Resistance

Resistance will inevitably arise while you're journaling because you'll start feeling emotions you don't want to feel.

We often numb those feelings with food, sex, drugs, TV—even by consuming self-help or spiritual entertainment (which was my jam). But leaning into your discomfort is how you go deep and the only way to truly change. Based on the early teachings of my mentor, spiritual leader, and *New York Times* best-selling author Gabrielle Bernstein's Recognize, Record, Release technique, the process below addresses resistance to unwanted feelings and forces you to bravely lean into them. I've seen the effectiveness of this process with countless clients. It truly is radical.

- **Action 1: Admit it.** When you hit resistance and want to stop writing, simply pause, take a breath, and recognize that there's something there for you to feel.

- **Action 2: Write it.** Write down in your journal whatever you're feeling. Just let it out onto the page.

- **Action 3: Dive into it.** Music is an amazing tool for deeply experiencing your feelings by bringing them to the surface and allowing them to release. So match what you're feeling to a song, and play it. If it's an angry feeling, listen to an angry song. If it's a melancholy feeling, listen to a sad song. If it's an ecstatic feeling, listen to an upbeat song, and so on. Allow yourself to dive into the emotion however you want to experience it. If you're compelled to get up and dance, do it; if you need to curl up and rock to it, then do that. Concentrate *solely* on the singular feeling you're dealing with, and allow it to rush through you—and out of you.

- **Action 4: Change it.** As soon as the song is over, grab your journal again. You've had that emotional release, and now you're ready to reach for a better feeling. From the new mental space you've created, freewrite (literally spew your every thought on the page) about any shifts in the feeling you had or how you want to change it. Just allow your pen to flow, and see what comes up.

Tip 3: Follow the Requirements

There are three main requirements to successfully let it out:

- **You have to believe.** The only way to heal is to believe you can heal.

- **You have to be patient.** Never push or force the process of discovering your feelings.

- **You have to befriend yourself.** Getting radically comfortable with yourself is the special sauce for making this process of self-study happen.

Requirement 1: Believe

I met one of my best friends online. Carly, a fellow blogger whom I admired, was one of my first guests on my podcast. We met live on the air and instantly became best friends, texting with emoticons all day like 12-year-olds and having deep Sunday chats like 80-year-old women. In one of these chats, she expanded on something she said on my podcast, which was, "If you believe Western medicine is going to heal you, it probably will. If you believe holistic healing is going to heal you, it probably will." That line stuck with me, but I didn't fully internalize it until months later when we were chatting in one of our long Sunday sessions.

We were both struggling with our skin. My body was going through a lot of changes internally, and externally it was manifesting in terrible, painful acne. Carly was having a similar experience. I was at such a low point; my skin was so bad that when I had the opportunity to go to the Wanderlust yoga festival in Copper Mountain, Colorado, for free—which would have been a dream come true—I turned it down because I was too embarrassed.

That night I called Carly and confided in her. I told her I was willing to leave my deep love for natural and holistic products and healing methods to go for a more aggressive, Western-medicine approach. I was also feeling pressure from my mom to see a dermatologist, but I had resisted going that route because I so badly wanted my skin to heal with the holistic methods I talked about on my blog. I had done my research on both, but nothing seemed to be working.

As Carly and I talked this all out like only close friends can do, she made me realize something profound: I didn't actually *believe* that either method would heal me. I doubted the traditional Western approach because there was part of me that deeply believed in holistic healing and didn't feel Western medicine was the route for me. On the other hand, I also didn't fully believe that an alternative holistic approach would work either, because somewhere within me I thought my mom and dermatologists were right, that this "natural stuff" wasn't strong enough to heal my acne.

When I discovered this conflict of beliefs, everything changed. I realized all I had to do was choose a method and *believe in it fully.* (There's even an exercise in this book based on exactly how I released my doubt around healing my condition.) I committed to holistically healing my skin and drew into my life all the people, support, and methods I needed, and, almost miraculously, my skin healed. It wasn't the method I chose that healed me; it was the fact I committed to believing in it. Western medicine could have easily healed me, too, if I was able to fully believe in that approach.

Belief is crucial, and you must have it to have success with the tools in this book. Believe they'll work for you, and they will. Believe they're silly and won't work for you, and they won't.

Requirement 2: Be Patient

In my story above, patience was essential to healing. While my skin was in the process of healing, I had to hold on to the belief that it would heal *even when* I couldn't see the results yet. If I had instead focused on the fact that my skin wasn't clear and become impatient, I would have taken action and messed with the process. Rather, I stayed grounded in my belief and let my body heal at its own pace.

So please: Apply patience to the tools in this book. You might need to take it slow, do an exercise more than once, or wait for the meaning to sink in after you write. Don't rush the process. The subtitle of this book is *A Journey through Journaling* for a reason. Cat's out of the bag, peeps—we all know it's about the journey, not the destination. Enjoy the ride. That's where the magic is.

Requirement 3: Befriend Yourself

You might likely feel that you know your best friends better than you know yourself. At least, that was the case for me. For most of my life, I didn't allow myself to authentically express who I was with other people—or even with myself—and I did this for so long that I lost touch with who that person even was. I found myself telling people what they wanted to hear, or saying only things that I felt they couldn't judge too harshly. To heal and come into my own, I had to get to know myself and befriend myself, just like I would a new friend. I did this with my journal.

I'd let out onto the page what I was actually thinking, not what I thought people wanted to hear. I'd write down my raw, real fears and insecurities, unafraid of people judging me for them. I'd write my authentic desires of what I truly wanted and dreamed up without fear of criticism. I never had to share my journal—it was completely for me, a place where I could express myself fully for the first time in my life. It was liberating.

Through letting out these thoughts, I could see the real me, not the watered-down chameleon I showed the world. I eventually began to like who I was. I was so much cooler when I was real!

I wanted to be friends with *me* more when I was real, and I realized that was probably what other people would value most about me, too. So I started to be "myself" more with others, and not just in my journal. I had found my voice through my journal. And while being real in my writing was the first step—I had to figure out on my own who I was before I could authentically express that to others—I ultimately had to befriend myself; I had to like my authentic self before I could ask anyone else to. With my new self-awareness and self-love, I could interact with the world in a more open, free-flowing, and authentic way. This is magnetizing. Trust me.

When I'm coaching clients, I'll often have them "date themselves" in our first few sessions. I'll guide them to quite literally take themselves out on a date, and advise they leave their phones behind and take only their journal as a companion. I'll have them go out somewhere, maybe to a park or a favorite coffee shop. I'll have them order a cup of tea and be fully present, just holding the hot cup in their hands, watching the steam, smelling it, observing the people around them—basically just noticing everything like they're Curious George. Then I have them write. They can write about themselves; they can write about what they see; they can write about how they relate to everything around them.

This exercise is powerful for getting out of your normal routine, as it prompts you to do something unique and be with yourself, fully and completely. A deep sense of self-awareness, I have found, is one of the true keys to happiness and fulfillment. So make sure to bring your real self, the self you've befriended, to your journal while you work through the tools in this book. If you feel you need a few getting-to-know-you dates before you begin, you have my full encouragement!

Tip 4: Cultivate Awareness

The goal of journaling isn't to make you into a "ball of sunshine" state 24/7. Rather, it is to give you tools to help shorten the time between coming out of the flow and going back into the flow—*flow* being that state where everything in your life seems to be moving effortlessly. We've all been there, and it's so awesome. Basically it looks something like this: You have a great hair day, you pick your outfit with ease, you get a nice text message and find the perfect parking spot, your favorite song is on the radio, and so on—that's "in the flow." Out of the flow is the opposite: You can't find anything to wear, your hair looks terrible, you get a mean text from your boss, you're late because you can't find a parking spot, and the song you hate keeps playing on the radio—that's what it's like to be "out of the flow."

While it seems like none of this is in your control, how you react to it definitely *is*. By choosing different thoughts during unpleasant situations, you can change your perceptions and shift from out of the flow to back in more quickly. *Awareness* of when you're out of the flow is the first step to getting back in alignment, and awareness can only happen in the present moment. When you feel out of alignment, you're in your "thinking mind." To get out of that, simply bring your attention to your feet—because they're farthest from your brain—and notice the moment you're currently in. The tools in this book will help you become more aware and present, because journaling requires it. Awareness is a muscle—these tools are your gym to help you develop it.

Tip 5: Be Radically Authentic and Honest

What stops us from feeling free and fully ourselves is what we are hiding: poor judgment calls we've made, things we're embarrassed about, goals of ours that seem too unrealistic to claim. We bury our dark secrets and get preoccupied managing them to ensure we don't appear less than perfect—or get caught in the lie of trying to appear perfect. But when we let it out (even if it's just to ourselves), we can breathe.

By being vulnerable and acknowledging what we're ashamed of, we let go of any guilt we're holding on to. As Brené Brown teaches, shame cannot survive being shared, and admitting our shame to ourselves is the first step.

So let's not waste your time. Make a commitment to radical authenticity and honesty when using the journaling tools in this book: Dig out the secrets you've buried, the things you're hiding, and show them the light of day by letting it all out on paper. If you're lying to yourself or writing what you think you "should" be writing or what someone else would want to read, stop yourself immediately, return to the present moment, and write what's true for you.

Tip 6: Fake It Till You Make It

When you're doing things that are new and uncomfortable, it's inevitable that to some extent you'll feel like you're pretending—at least I always do. When I started teaching yoga, I felt like I wasn't *actually* a yoga teacher but just pretending to be one, mimicking my own teachers. But as Kurt Vonnegut says in *Mother Night,* "We are what we pretend to be, so we must be careful about what we pretend to be." Basically, he's saying that it works to fake it till you make it. You will feel like a fraud, but so does everyone else.

The process of journaling and expressing your feelings honestly on paper might be brand-new for you. If that's the case, going this deep might cause some strong reactions:

a) Wanting to stop or quit

b) Feeling like you're a fraud

c) Thinking you're wasting your time

d) Turning off your new, heightened awareness and zoning out in familiar, comfortable habits— watching TV, reading magazines, browsing online—anything to avoid that new feeling

Don't let that stop you. *Everyone* feels as though they're pretending when they start a new routine. When you haven't done something before, or you haven't done it consistently, it's not ingrained yet. This new way of expressing your feelings fully, as a writer, is uncomfortable. You might be feeling like a ball of emotion when you begin this process because perhaps you rarely ever allow yourself to feel your uncomfortable emotions. And feeling uncomfortable is when most people quit.

So when you reach this point, you must ask yourself: *Do I want to have a deep life? Do I want to feel the richness of mad love and the sadness of heartbreak? Do I want to feel the full spectrum of emotions . . . or do I want to numb out?* Journaling is a practice that puts a mirror right up to your face. It shows you what's going on at a deeper level when you allow yourself to examine your feelings as they authentically flow out of you.

When you feel like you're playing pretend as a writer but you *like what you're pretending*—that's when you need to keep going. That's when, with time, the routine becomes ingrained, and before you know it . . . you will no longer be pretending.

Setting Up for Success

Before I let you go to the tool-kit section of this book and you let your pen run wild, I have a few quick notes. The tool kit holds a collection of various exercises, activities, freewriting prompts, and list-making and organizational tools that you can do in any order. As I mentioned at the start of this manual, you can approach the journaling tools chronologically or flip to whichever tool you feel is most relevant to you on a certain day. Or, of course, there's always the unique option of letting the Universe decide by randomly opening to a page.

There are 55 journaling tools in all; I chose that number intentionally for its symbolic meaning of changing your old ways and starting anew, which I learned from Doreen Virtue's work. The tools are organized into seven meaningful categories—from getting going to getting organized, to finding presence, creating abundance, and inviting in healing. They are yours to change, personalize, and put your own unique spin on.

These tools can be your companion everywhere. (My favorite time to journal is actually on a plane, as I feel my consciousness and clarity heighten as my altitude does.) Take as long as you need with each one. They will be there whenever you need them, and the beauty is that you can return to them over and over again—and in fact, you should. They're designed to be fluid and to be repeated as you develop. Your answers will be different each time because *you* are a different person each time, and you'll have new things that need to be let out of you. It's like taking the garbage out: Having done it once, you're not done for the rest of your life. Rather, because you accumulate more over time, you must continually dispose.

Most important, the journaling tools are impossible to do incorrectly, unless you simply fail to try.

What You'll Need

School-supply shopping was my favorite part of the fall, and I still get nostalgic come late August when I see the colorful store displays of backpacks, markers, and folders that used to be Lisa Frank unicorns but are now One Direction's and Taylor Swift's faces. I always indulge myself with some new office supplies at the start of fall. I invite you to invest in a few items at the outset of your journaling practice that will inspire and get you excited about this process, much in the same way a new pencil kit or folder collection set you up for success in elementary school.

This book is not a workbook, so you'll need to invest in a separate journal as a companion to this book. Picking up this book was an act of self-care. I suggest that you continue that effort by investing in a journal you love—perhaps something from Shinola, Anthropologie, Moleskine, or your favorite stationery store or bookshop. While a single journal or notebook should offer plenty of room to do the tools, I suggest starting to collect journals so that you can devote different journals to different techniques or times of day. For instance, I have my morning journal; my gratitude and evening journal; and my on-the-go, lightweight, portable journal that I take with me everywhere.

Pay attention to all the details of the journal that you're selecting—how it feels in your hands, how it flips from page to page, and most important how *you* feel holding it. Your journal is your sidekick on this journey, so make sure it's something you love to be around frequently. You can get a journal basically anywhere these days, and while of course Amazon .com can have one to you in a few clicks, I suggest going out and selecting one in person, if possible.

Here are some of my favorite places to get my journals (I'm somewhat of a hoarder when it comes to them):

— **Bookstores**. My heart rate instantly lowers when I walk into a bookstore, so anytime there's an excuse for me to go to one, I'll take it. Most bookstores have a wide variety of journals, including the classic brand **Moleskine**, so you're sure to have a vast selection to choose from.

— **Anthropologie.** This is one of my favorite stores in general (sometimes I like to pretend I live in their home section—anyone else do that?), but their sale section is especially effective for picking up some really beautiful journals, often with big discounts. Anthropologie carries some of my favorite paper-goods brands like **Rifle Paper Co.**, and it's always fun to wander the store. Their journals make the best gifts, too, and hey, enlisting a friend to go through this book with you and let it out alongside you could be the special sauce for really enjoying the process.

— **Little independent shops.** Who doesn't love exploring tiny, independent shops while visiting new places? Well I sure do, and buying unique journals in places I'm traveling to and exploring is always extra meaningful. When I purchase one, I think about the internal exploration that will occur on the blank pages; and as I flip through it, I imagine the vast words, lists, and *aha* moments that will soon fill those pages.

— **Shinola.** I have to shout out to one of my favorite brands, **Shinola.** I live in Detroit, where Shinola was founded, and while the company's known for their handmade bikes and watches, their handcrafted journals are what really get me in the door. Shinola's durable, high-quality journals are produced using paper sourced from sustainably managed North American forests. I feel all professional when I'm using mine and like to pretend I'm Hemingway as I write in it.

— **Office-supply stores.** Go here for legal pads. Yes, you read that correctly—I'm talking about those yellow, rectangular, lined pads that flip vertically. Legal pads have actually been where some of my best, most brilliant ideas and insights have been let out of me. In all honesty, the entire idea for this book and many of the tools in it were written out early mornings on yellow legal pads. I kid you not. Like, I could show you photos.

Now, it may seem contradictory to all the suggestions above to have a not-so-aesthetically-pleasing, much cheaper option among all these beautiful ones, but there's a method in my madness. When I started coaching clients one-on-one on my journaling process and taking them through many of the tools in this book, I would send them a welcome package in the mail with a beautiful journal like the ones above. What I realized after a while was that they were writing in that journal what they thought I wanted to hear, *not what they needed to say.* They were filling beautiful journals with beautiful words . . . but sometimes letting it out is *messy.* And messy writing is often the most healing writing.

With a legal pad, there's no pressure to make your words as beautiful as the journal itself. The legal pad allows the words to just be what they are—crossed out, messy, negative, raw, fearful—which is part of the process of getting to the other side. By writing on a legal pad, or simply lineless computer paper, you'll be able to be authentic and reckless with your words, which is necessary in this process. So for some of these tools, you might want to toss aside your pretty journal and write on something a little more rugged, like a legal pad.

In addition to your journal(s), following is your complete list of supplies.

Supplies for Successfully Letting It Out

- An open mind
- Your curiosity
- A favorite journal or notebook
- A legal pad or computer paper
- A favorite writing instrument

Although nothing else is required, the following are some "nice to haves":

- A comfortable, quiet place (Again, not required! The journaling prompts can be done anywhere, from an airplane to a crowded car ride, and you'll be surprised where the best info comes through.)
- A cup of tea
- A burning candle
- Calm, soft, inspiring music

This is the point where I wish you well on your journey through journaling. Know that it's one with many twists and turns—some surprising, some cathartic, some deliciously uncomfortable, and all incredibly rewarding. And as I mentioned earlier, because *you* are a new person each and every day, these tools can never be exhausted; your journey is an endless discovery that keeps getting better and better the more you use and return to each tool. And, of course, your traveling companion is *yourself*. The good news is, as with any travel companion, you'll get to know them better the more time you spend together, and I predict you'll start liking who you are more and more. And of course I'll be there, too, guiding you every step of the way. The route is mapped out for you, you're set up for success, so let's go let it out. Bon voyage!

JOURNALING TOOL KIT

PART I

LET IT OUT TO GET GOING

From Zero to Flow

"When the time is on you, start, and the pressure will be off."
— YOGI BHAJAN

Have you ever woken up with a to-do list a mile long, but you're so lost as to where to begin that you just do nothing? Do you ever feel so overwhelmed by midday that everything just comes to a screeching halt? Or maybe you've felt the blahs, totally underwhelmed with the day ahead, and lost the motivation to even get out of bed? Yeah, me, too.

Even when our tasks are fun, quick, and trivial, we put them off merely because there are so many. Regardless of how long or short your task list is, beginning is often the hardest part. But once you start and get in the flow, it's smooth sailing and easy to keep going. Think of how it feels when you're on a roll while cleaning, e-mailing, or cooking: Time flies by and what you're doing feels effortless and like you could go forever. You've probably been in the flow many times before—the trick is getting *into* it.

When a nasty bout of procrastination hits, just doing something—anything!—to grab your focus will automatically make you feel productive and build momentum to continue. This section of tools is designed to get you into that awesome flow state.

Follow the directions and use these tools anytime to get back into the flow. To avoid overwhelming yourself with too much at once, I suggest doing one tool per sitting; this helps ensure that the tools *themselves* don't wind up feeling like extra tasks that add stress. Many of the tools in this section have become part of my own personal practice that I use often. Approach them as you would a buffet: Don't gorge on everything all at once; rather, try them all, one at a time, and then take what you like best and leave the rest.

- 01 The Morning Dump
- 02 The Dream Decoder
- 03 The Getting Started Pages
- 04 The Creativity Muscle Toner
- 05 The Excitement List
- 06 The Opposite Experiment
- 07 The Productivity Pivot

THE MORNING DUMP

This tool is a mainstay in any journaler's practice. It's a real game changer that you can return to again and again. On some mornings, the first step for me is long, but once I get the thoughts clouding my mind written down, I have new clarity, and rad ideas begin to come through by the third or fourth page. On other mornings, I don't have as much to say and it's merely a few words.

Think of the first step of this exercise as emotional mouthwash—rinsing all the gook you woke up with out of your mind. Using it first thing in the morning, just after coming out of your dream state, is extra powerful—you have the most access to your subconscious mind when you first awaken. By dumping your thoughts, you're skimming the icky scum off the surface of your mind so that you can get to the clean water underneath. By not scraping off those thoughts first thing, you may never see the new, clear, creative thoughts under the scum barrier.

This exercise uses a similar concept to the morning pages of Julia Cameron's book *The Artist's Way*, which she says "provoke, clarify, comfort, cajole, prioritize and synchronize the day at hand." What a lovely description. Morning pages, and particularly my creative personal-spin exercise below, have dramatically improved my life by giving me greater self-awareness, since I am able to begin each day with a clear picture of where my thoughts are.

Directions:

- *Step 1:* **Dump it out.** (No, not *that* kind of dump.) In the morning right when you wake up, let out anything that's on your mind. Flood the page with your thoughts, worries, ideas, and dreams. It doesn't matter if it doesn't make sense. Simply make sure that everything you write is honest and authentic, regardless of quality. You can make yourself fill the whole page or simply write down just a few things. This step skims the scum off the top of your mind pond so that you can get to the clear water underneath—*new* thoughts, rather than the ones you think on repeat.

- *Step 2:* **Connect to gratitude.** With your new mental openness, write down five things you're grateful for—the first things that come to your mind. Connecting to gratitude right away is crucial, because when you focus on the positive aspects of what you have, you create more of what you want.

- *Step 3:* **Declare your deepest desires.** We often don't allow ourselves to actually want what we want, since we might be afraid that by declaring our dreams, the pressure's on to make them happen. However, if you announce to the Universe what you really want, you're placing an order for it to happen—effortlessly. So write down what you want to manifest *today*. Make this statement in the present tense. You could say, "I receive an unexpected, new source of income," or "I enter a new loving relationship." Just simply write down the thing that sounds the best to you this particular morning.

- *Step 4:* **Visualize.** Once your thoughts have all been dumped onto the page, you've connected to gratitude, and you've allowed yourself to declare what you desire, for at least one minute sit in stillness and visualize what it would be like for your deepest desires to manifest into form. Get extremely specific here. In your mind, create images and stories of the life you dream of. For instance, if you manifest a loving, supportive relationship, how would you feel in it? If you manifest a new source of income, who would you tell about it, how would you use it, and most important, how would it make you *feel*? When you visualize, you create a mental imprint—and if you've been there in your mind, it becomes easier to go there in your body. And then . . .

- *Step 5:* **Completely let it go.** After your brief visualization, return to the present moment and gently let go of the mental image of what you want to manifest. It helps to write down in your journal this powerful releasing statement: "I let go, I allow, and I trust this is happening on my behalf today. Thank you, it is already done, and I am grateful in advance." Just like no one wants to date someone who is constantly clinging, your dreams won't manifest if you are clinging to them. When you let them go, you allow the Universe to conspire on your behalf to bring them into your life.

This exercise is powerful. When I was teaching it one day in a workshop, I used the simple example of manifesting $100 of unexpected income. Later that day, exactly $100 of unexpected income deposited into my account. During my workshop someone had made a $100 donation to my podcast. That might not happen every time, but I've seen this sort of thing occur time and again in my clients' lives as well. Keep in mind, too, that even if it seems nothing physically manifested that day, that doesn't mean it didn't start to. For instance, you could have briefly met someone who will become your partner; however, the relationship won't begin until weeks later. Be open to things coming to you in perfect timing, which might not be when you think. Simply let go, allow, and enjoy your day, knowing you started it with a powerful practice.

TOOL NO. 02

THE DREAM DECODER

Have you ever woken up from an amazing dream, one where the emotions that dream evoked in you set the entire day on a happy path? Isn't it the *best* when that happens? Dreams are powerful, and this tool will help you unleash some of that power and use it more deliberately by guiding you to use your dreams for information. According to the teachings of Abraham (an entity of Spirits facilitated by Esther Hicks, whom I'm super inspired by, as far-out as it may seem), it's easier to manifest in your dream state. Abraham teaches that while in our physical reality manifestations take time, the manifestations in our dream state are immediate—that is, your dreams are *an advanced announcement* of what's manifesting with your current thoughts.

This tool guides you to use your dreams as a preview of where your thoughts are taking you. The good part about dreams is that it is much easier to recover from your manifestations in the sleep state than in physical reality. For instance, a broken leg in a dream state is much easier to recover from than one in your physical reality, but the meaning behind the broken leg in your dream can clue you in to something deeper going on in your life.

Recurring or similar dreams, according to Abraham, mean that you are on the brink of a manifestation similar to the dream. This doesn't mean that the exact situation will pop into your reality, but that you'll manifest something that *feels* of the same vibration—unless you shift your vibration, which is totally possible, and journaling is a fabulous way to do that.

Directions:

- *Step 1:* Keep your journal by your bed. Before you go to sleep, make it your intention to remember your dreams; then immediately upon waking, write down anything you can remember about your dreams. Don't obsess about details; even a few notes will do. It's important to do this immediately upon rising because we all know how quickly we forget our dreams—within minutes, poof, they start to dissipate from our minds . . .

- *Step 2:* After getting all your notes down about what happened in your dream, freewrite for two to five minutes about how the dream made you *feel.* Focus both on how you felt *in the dream* and how you're feeling about it *now,* back in a conscious state.

- *Step 3:* If the dream felt good and brought up positive vibrations, acknowledge that, and freewrite on ways you can stay in that vibration for the rest of the day. If the dream felt uncomfortable or jarring in any way, ask yourself what in your life might be creating a similar feeling of being unsettled or uncomfortable, and freewrite on how you can shift the vibration you're in. Remember, your dreams are barometers of your thoughts and the vibration they're creating. By tuning in to how the dream made you feel, you can choose whether you want to stay in that feeling or shift it.

THE GETTING STARTED PAGES

Sitting down and forcing yourself into your workday will only get you so far. You could have your ideal dream job, but there will still be moments in the daily grind where you won't want to get started—that's what separates work from hobbies. With hobbies, you always have a choice if and when you want to do them; but with work or your career, sometimes you'll have to get the job done regardless of whether you're feeling inspired to. So when you find yourself sitting down to do your work and not feeling into it, this exercise can help you get going.

Instead of reaching for inspiration (and, let's be real, probably procrastinating for hours), ease into your workday by writing. By letting out whatever you're feeling in the moment, you open space for creative possibilities and solutions to come through—and most of all, you get present: You don't let the drama of last night or the stress of this morning or the anticipation of the upcoming evening get in the way. And, as I said earlier, we tend to think the same set of thoughts on repeat all day long—so if you can let those out, you'll create space for brilliance.

Directions:

- *Step 1:* Directly upon getting to your desk, studio, or workbench, open a fresh document or turn to a blank page. Write down everything on your mind and how you're feeling about the tasks ahead. This might include making a task list of what you need to do, and what would make you feel accomplished at the end of your workday. Or you could simply write about your resistance to getting to work. Just write whatever is true for you in the moment. Limit yourself to *no more than* 15 minute of journaling, as any more time spent turns this from a productive exercise into straight-up procrastination.

- *Step 2:* After you've acknowledged your resistance to getting going and/or organized your tasks so you know where to focus that day, put away your journal and get to work. Once you've accomplished something, revisit your journal and quickly jot down how it feels to have that task complete. Check in with yourself on a break, and if you return to your work feeling over- or underwhelmed, redo the process to address that resistance.

THE CREATIVITY MUSCLE TONER

This tool was inspired by *Alice in Wonderland*. One of my favorite quotes from its sequel, *Through the Looking-Glass*, is, "Why, sometimes I've believed as many as six impossible things before breakfast." This is wise and inspiring, because the rational side of your brain *is* more forgiving first thing in the morning, therefore allowing you to be more creative.

We all have creativity within us just like we all have muscles. And creativity *is* just like a muscle; you have to work it to build it. If you get into the habit of thinking creatively, it will become easier and easier, and eventually, when you find yourself in a situation where you need to think of ideas quickly—in business or with your family, for instance—you will be able to with ease. By working your creativity muscle every morning, you'll not only tone and expand your creative capacity, but you'll also build an idea bank you can have on hand.

We all came into this world with creativity. When people say they aren't creative, it simply means they haven't been working their creativity muscle. You never see a child looking at a blank coloring page, paralyzed by which color crayon to pick up, or looking at a set of Legos, unsure of how to start building. Of course not—they just create.

If you're still uncertain, then take the word of acclaimed author Elizabeth Gilbert, who talks about creativity beautifully. She explains that humans are *inherently* meant to be creative creatures; our physiology allows for it, from our ability to think deeply and feel emotions, to our dream state that we spend a third of our lives in. More so than any other species, we have the ideal circumstances for inspiration and creativity to set up camp; therefore, it's our obligation to use it. We might have kept our creativity locked up after the age of about eight or nine and think it has genuinely dissipated, but that's impossible. *Creativity is deep within our DNA.*

So think of this tool as CrossFit for your creative mind; it will help you unleash your creativity. And the more you apply it, the more natural using your creative muscle will become. One last tip: Having fun is the key to creativity!

Directions:

Part 1

- *Step 1:* Complete your morning ritual, whatever that means for you, starting the day in an intentional way. Take time to tune yourself to the day through prayer, movement, meditation, freewriting your Morning Dump (Tool No. 01), and/or enjoying your morning cup of tea or coffee.

- *Step 2:* Once you've taken time to wake up and tune in, and prior to starting any tasks for the day, write down three to five unique, imaginative ideas. These *aren't* to-do list items; it doesn't matter what they're about or if you will even follow through on them. Think simply of the guidance from Wonderland—"impossible things"—and don't limit yourself at all. They can be ideas to help someone, to surprise your friends, to do a random act of kindness; they can be ideas for your garden, for your business, or for someone else's business; they can be ideas about trips you could take, stories you could write, movies to watch, routines to start, or recipes to cook. Again, it doesn't matter what you write about—this tool is about working the creativity muscle when your mind is fresh and hasn't been clouded by the day yet.

Part 2

This part isn't necessarily something to be done daily, but definitely every weekend. Think of it like a weekend brunch type of tool—something you'd do on a leisurely Saturday or Sunday or whenever you have a bit more time to spend with your journal.

- *Step 1:* Think of a story from your life. It could be recent, or it could be from years ago or from childhood; it could be funny or ludicrous, or it could be dramatic and serious.

- *Step 2:* Write it out, just as if you were to tell it to a friend. Simply write what happened. Transcribe it the same way you would speak it, using as much detail and description as you can. If you can't remember all the details, simply make some up—you have full creative license.

- *Step 3:* Great! Now you have a rough draft for your story. Now, go back through and <u>underline</u> things that weren't interesting, and make notes on how you could replace them. Perhaps you make a twist ending or add in a new character, and really shake up the entire trajectory of the story. This is your time to use your imagination—let it run wild.

- *Step 4:* Set a timer for 10 minutes, and rewrite the same story with all your imaginative add-ins from Step 3. Pretend you're a professional writer composing your story for *The New Yorker* (in fact, you might as well submit it—what's the harm?) and really get into it. Just have a blast allowing your creativity to flow, perhaps for the first time in years. Use this tool whenever you need a little creative-writing boot camp.

- *Bonus step:* Take your story from Step 4 and either print it out or rip it out. Then head to your local bookstore, find another copy of this book, and insert your story into this page in that book. It will give the next reader a nice surprise and will add an appendix of entertaining fiction to this very practical nonfiction work you're holding in your hands.

THE EXCITEMENT PLAN

Have you ever struggled with pressing the snooze button multiple times before finally getting out of bed? Remember what it was like to wake up as a child on Christmas morning, when you were just so excited to be awake? You didn't struggle even for a second to get up. This tool brings you back to that excitement—it'll help catapult you out of bed in the morning. Focusing on what you're looking forward to will help it become the first thing you think about when you open your eyes, pulling you out of bed and getting you going in the morning.

When I first started using this tool, I found myself looking forward to mornings in a way I never had before. I'd be excited to go to sleep early so it could be morning again, just like I felt on Christmas Eve as a kid. I began to relish my simple alone time in the early hours of the day when most of the world is still sleeping—it felt like my own magical time. I wanted to wake up because the morning I had planned was better than my dreams. As clichéd as that sounds, I think the goal of "living the life of your dreams" is finding that excitement to bound out of bed and experience the day, rather than staying asleep and pressing snooze.

Directions:

- *Step 1:* Set your alarm 10 minutes early in the morning (make sure to go to bed 10 minutes sooner, of course), and in that time you set aside for yourself, do something special in the early hours of the day, before anyone else around you wakes up. Perhaps brew a new flavor of tea and read a short story from an anthology (do one per morning); or put on a dim light or rock lamp and do some yoga while listening to your new favorite song; or pop in your headphones to listen to the new episode of your favorite podcast or the next chapter of the audiobook you're really into—but whatever it is, *it can't seem like work.* If the first thing you're doing when you get out of bed is a grueling ab workout or tedious paperwork, leaping from your covers is going to be the last thing you want to do. So do yourself a favor and give yourself 10 minutes of pure pleasure when you wake up.

- *Step 2:* Plan this out the night before in your journal, and even write it down on a note beside your bed to remind you of your morning intention. It might be the same thing daily, but also leave room for it to change day to day. What feels fun one morning might seem like a chore another, so check in each night and write at least one thing that will thrill you enough to want to get out of bed.

For instance, one of my friends wakes up consistently 10 minutes earlier than her boyfriend so she can sit on the kitchen floor and drink her coffee. It's a simple ritual with herself that she loves and it sets the tone for her day. You don't have to adapt her ritual or any of mine; rather, create your own and allow it to change and expand day to day, week to week, and season to season based on what excites you. Maybe an extra 10 minutes will turn into 30 as you come to cherish that time in the mornings alone. No matter the case, getting out of bed will become easier and easier.

THE OPPOSITE
EXPERIMENT

There's an episode of *Seinfeld* I remember watching as a kid with my dad, where the character George decides to do everything opposite for a day. With the help of his friends, he comes to the conclusion that every decision he's made so far in his life has gotten him to the stagnant place he's at, and since he wants his life to be different, he decides to literally flip every choice he makes and do the *exact opposite.* He starts by ordering the opposite of his usual meal, and his antics even include going up to talk to a beautiful woman and being completely honest with her about the fact that he's unemployed and lives with his parents, rather than lying to make himself appear more attractive to her. By doing the opposite of everything he normally does, George starts to see the infinite possibilities he was previously unaware of when he was stuck in his mundane routines.

That episode inspired this tool. It guides you to shake things up and make the opposite choice than you normally would, and notice the shifts that take place as a result. By simply switching up your routines, you may discover new insights you might have missed before.

Einstein is said to have defined insanity as doing the same thing over and over again and expecting a different result. So from that I infer the opposite to be true: Doing things differently over and over again will result in unique perspectives and new, exciting opportunities.

Directions:

- *Step 1:* Decide on a time period to try this experiment. Give yourself anywhere from a day to a weekend to a full week (if you have the guts!) where you'll commit to doing the opposite of all the things you normally do. Write in your journal the new things you'll try, and add to the list as you go along and think of new things. For instance, you'll take alternative routes to work or school, you'll order new things at restaurants, you'll go to sleep early if you usually stay up late, you'll try tea instead of coffee or vice versa, you'll walk instead of run, and so on.

  Tailor this experiment to you, and be sure to not overthink it. Allow it to be uncomfortable and embrace it; remember, this is simply a temporary experiment, so after you complete the time frame you committed to, you can return to your normal routines again.

- *Step 2:* For the duration of the experiment, also document all the new things you're noticing from simply switching up your routines and trying something new. Jot down notes about how you're feeling throughout—notice any discomfort, how much you feel you cling to your routines, and how difficult you're finding it to let go of them even for a little while (that was the case for me at least). Also, see if you feel liberated and excited to try new things as well.

- *Step 3:* Once the experiment is completed, reflect on the entire experience in your journal. What did you learn? Did you notice anything about yourself? Are there any routines that actually felt good to release.that you don't want to pick up again? Are there any new things you tried that you want to continue? Do you want to continue keeping things fresh and *still* do the opposite of what you'd been doing? Write about whatever comes up about your experience—and repeat this tool whenever you're feeling a bit stagnant in your life.

THE PRODUCTIVITY PIVOT

When we fall off the wagon into "bad day mode," our tendency is often to keep going down that dirt road and call the rest of the day a wash. Our mental talk might be something like: *I've already done nothing today, so I might as well just order pizza . . . and stay in my jammies . . . and binge watch that new show on Netflix.* This sneaky tool shifts your energy when you're overwhelmed, uninspired, or feeling like you're headed in a negative direction.

Noticing the good in your day automatically pulls you out of a downward spiral, which can so easily suck you in deeper and deeper if you don't step in and change course. Doing this tool can immediately save the day from spinning out of control, before it becomes too difficult to pull out of. While one day of laziness might be restful, *days* of laziness sink you further into their quicksand and will require more work and tools to pull out of.

This tool nips laziness in the bud by helping you pivot your energy back to a positive vibe immediately and not allow things to get worse. Even if your entire day so far was spent in a funk, you can shift out of that at any moment. No, you don't have to wait until the next morning—just do this tool! Even if it's 6 P.M. or later, the day is not over yet. You can pivot your day into a productive one, even if it didn't begin that way.

Directions:

- *Step 1:* Write at the top of your page: "Things I'm Loving Right Now." Begin the list by jotting down the few things that come to your mind. Here is my example as I'm writing this:

  1. The soup I just had for lunch

  2. My friend

  3. My ukulele

  4. The new album I downloaded

  5. The dream I had last night

  6. That TED Talk I watched

- *Step 2:* Halfway down the page and underneath your list from Step 1, leaving some room to grow the top list, write: "Things I Want to Change." Begin noting everything that comes to mind, letting it drain out of you.

  1. My negative perceptions of my body

  2. Feeling like I don't have enough time

  3. The cold weather

- *Step 3:* Look at the "Things I Want to Change" list from Step 2, and count how many items are on it. For every item on that list, add an additional item to "Things I'm Loving Right Now."

- *Step 4:* Notice the fact that the former list is longer than the latter. Feel your gratitude for the things you're loving, and work on creating more things for that list—things you enjoy, things that make you feel accomplished and proud of yourself. Keep adding until you feel better.

- *Step 5:* After you feel better and your mood lifts (even slightly is all that's needed), turn to a fresh page in your journal and write one final, short list: "Three Things I'll Accomplish Tonight." Keep it to no more than three items, and keep them simple. The point is not to overwhelm yourself with tasks but to give yourself a few actionable things you can look forward to that will pivot you into productivity and set the day in a new direction. It can be as simple as this:

1. Bake that sweet potato for dinner; I'll add tons of cinnamon (yum).

2. While it's in the oven, do 15 minutes of an online yoga class.

3. After dinner, take a shower and listen to a podcast while I organize everything for the next day, and head to bed early.

LET IT OUT TO GET ORGANIZED

Declutter Your Mind, Declutter Your Life

"Getting organized is a sign of self-respect."
— GABRIELLE BERNSTEIN

Has feeling overwhelmed ever gotten the best of you? We all juggle so much, and sometimes getting it down on paper is the only way to know where to even begin to make a dent. However, even *that* can seem overwhelming. Do you wish that you could have a professional organizer hack your mind and carefully place everything you need to take care of in beautifully organized compartments for you to focus on, one at a time? Well, the truth is that no one can organize your thoughts, desires, or goals like you can.

I'm here to guide you in decluttering your mind so that you can see what's most important—versus what can probably wait. We'll use your feelings and desires as your road map to lead you to where you should spend your time. The techniques in this section will work wonders in helping you find the clarity to lay out what needs to be done, be more productive, and take things one step at a time. You'll discover your "time leaks" and patch those up until you're using every second of your time in a healthy way—one that's in line with your goals.

Organization is preventive medicine for overwhelm. And getting organized doesn't have to be a chore. In fact, it shouldn't be, or you won't do it. Organizing your day, week, month, and even your meals or your home or wardrobe should be an enjoyable experience that makes you feel expansive and powerful. The tools in this section will not only make you excited to be organized but also make the entire process fun.

So let's let it out and organize it, shall we?

- 08 The Daily Feeling Action List
- 09 The Self-Care Weekly Outlook
- 10 The Monthly Manifesto
- 11 The Fridge-to-Plate Meal Planner
- 12 The Clutter Clearer
- 13 The Prioritizer

THE DAILY FEELING ACTION LIST

This is a radical way to remix your daily to-do list in order to reflect how you want to *feel,* rather than what you want to accomplish. Have you ever completed a full to-do list only to still feel completely unfulfilled? Or have you ever reached a goal and not felt what you were anticipating from achieving it? That's because check marks on to-do lists are not what you need to feel fulfilled—instead, chase the feeling.

As author Danielle LaPorte teaches, your desires and feelings are your prayers, inspiring and leading you to where you're meant to go. (Check out her teachings for how to develop your "core desired feelings" for your life.) With this tool, you'll check in daily with how you're feeling and how you'd *like* to feel that day. Once you determine your single aspirational "feeling word" for the day, it's easy to clearly define actions you'll take to feel that way throughout it. It doesn't matter whether you check them all off; they're merely ideas to move you in the direction of your desire. Having a single, pointed feeling to chase every day rather than simply a to-do list is crucial to this tool. Let that one feeling guide every decision you make that day.

Directions:

- *Step 1:* In the morning, select a single "feeling word" that clearly describes how you want to feel for the day ahead. Choose just one word. Trust that the first word that pops into your mind is right, and write across the top of your journal page, "Today I want to feel [insert your word]."

- *Step 2:* Under your word, list 5 to 10 *action items* you'll take that day to help you feel that way. For instance, if your feeling word is *energized,* perhaps you'll list: *Go to the gym, Eat a salad with protein,* and *Take frequent breaks for a brisk walk outside,* to name a few. If your word of the day is *relaxed,* you might put down: *Get a massage, Drink hot chamomile tea on my break,* and *Listen to chill instrumental music.* It's that simple.

THE SELF-CARE WEEKLY OUTLOOK

Self-care is your responsibility, yet most of us tend to not treat it as seriously as other responsibilities and obligations we have to those around us. Perhaps it feels selfish or even self-indulgent to spend time on your own self-care, but I'm going to go out on a limb here and argue that it's actually the *opposite*—that by *not* engaging in your own self-care, you're not allowing yourself to show up fully as your best self for those who need you . . . and that's actually pretty selfish.

To really show up for other people, for your work or your craft, and even for inspiration, you have to first serve yourself mentally and physically. This tool allows your weeks to have balance between serving yourself and serving others. By penciling in self-care action items as you would your other obligations, your weeks become a more even mix. The excitement will outweigh any dread, and it will even lessen the discomfort of the commitments that you're not as thrilled about by giving you things to look forward to.

Directions:

- *Step 1:* Set aside a time at the beginning of each new week, perhaps on Sunday night or Monday morning, to check in with yourself about the week ahead. Create a column for each day of the week across your journal page with the date labeled at the top.

- *Step 2:* Look at your calendar and fill in everything you have scheduled for the week on your page. Get the bare bones down first: your scheduled appointments, commitments, and duties. Even though you have this in your calendar, it helps to write it out and see it all in one place in front of you—and this is crucial for the next step.

- *Step 3:* Circle anything that you're *not* looking forward to. Don't question why; just notice how seeing it written down makes you feel. Immediately after circling these items, see if there's any way you can get out of any of them, since they're clearly not serving you in some way. This may not be feasible for some items (e.g., funerals, work meetings, doctor's appointment, and the like), and that's no problem; in fact, it means you'll have more to work with in Step 4.

- *Step 4:* For every item that you circled and can't get out of, add an item somewhere else in the week that you *are* looking forward to: a self-care action like taking a bath, getting a massage, calling a best friend, or going shopping. Pencil it in as a nonnegotiable.

- *Step 5:* Add one additional self-care item somewhere in the week ahead, making sure that there are more self-care actions than obligations.

THE MONTHLY MANIFESTO

When life picks up to high speed throughout the busy week, you sometimes don't have time to think about what you need in order to feel your desired state of being—with this monthly manifesto, though, it's all set out for you. You can nourish your body with love and do exactly what you desire *without* having to think about what you want to engage in. It'll all be mapped out for you, so you can merely execute. Just consult the collage you will have created, where it's lovingly waiting.

Completing this tool ensures you have all the time, space, materials, ingredients, and resources to embody your single, pointed intention for the month and to follow through on how you want to *feel* for the month. Remember that the manifesto you create is a guide to inspire, *not* something to follow rigidly. Perhaps new things will come in, and you can add them as you go. Inspiration is endless, so be open.

Directions:

Every month, create a collage or visual collection of goals centered on how you want to *feel*. It must be deeply personal and specific. It can start as a list in your journal and remain a list, *or* you can get crafty and pick up some poster board and add color, photos, and magazine clippings. Either way, it should be a visual, organized reminder of actions you're intending to take this month in order to feel how you want to feel.

Here are ideas of what to include (again, personalize for how you want to *feel*):

- A single, pointed intention, as in: "I want to feel [fill in here—energized, productive, free, etc.]"

- Photos that make you feel really juicy and fulfilled in the moment

- Quotes and mantras you'd like to focus on

- Addresses or pictures of places you want to go, things you want to do, and when you will do them

- Recipes for food you want to eat, what you need for them, and when you will create them

- Videos you want to watch

- Podcasts you look forward to listening to

- Phone calls you're excited to make

- Classes you want to try

- Meditations you want to do

- Books you want to focus on

- Things you want to create

- People you want to hang out with

- Albums or playlists you want to listen to
- Movies or TV shows you want to watch

Note: This will be a practical, organized place for you to firm up what you will focus on. Be sure that you choose just a few things each month, so as not to overwhelm yourself. The goal is to feel "whelmed" by your manifesto, not overwhelmed. Remember—there is always another month.

THE FRIDGE-TO-PLATE MEAL PLANNER

How often are you standing in front of a fully stocked fridge, tummy rumbling, thinking, *I have nothing to eat!* And how often does the food in your fridge go bad without you even realizing it? The fridge can be a black hole for the food you come home with. It goes in, you forget what you bought, and eventually you pull it out, green, fuzzy, and sad, no longer excited to eat what it has become.

This tool is a helpful, practical tracker allowing you to stay organized with the food you have on hand. With it on the fridge, you won't have to do any rummaging or searching; rather, you'll clearly see all the contents of your fridge as well as ideas for meals you were excited to make. Unlike a strict meal plan, this tool promotes fluidity and intuitive eating by encouraging you to choose what you want to eat in the moment rather than what you plotted out days in advance. Making true intuitive food choices requires access and therefore a well-stocked kitchen. Basically, intuitive eating is relearning how to hear and respond to innate hunger and fullness cues. (If you want to know more, check out the book

Intuitive Eating, by Evelyn Tribole and Elyse Resch.) While the concept seems simple, for chronic dieters like myself it can take some learning.

I realized listening to my body's cravings goes out the window when I'm starving, and I'll choose the quickest and easiest food I see. This tool reminds you in your hungry moments what options you have, allowing you to reach for what your body desires rather than the nearest piece of fruit on the counter when you really wanted a substantial meal. I use this tool and a little planning to have a variety of diverse options on hand so I can make intuitive choices when hunger strikes.

Directions:

- *Step 1:* As soon as you get home from the grocery store and put away your newly purchased food items, take out your receipt and transcribe the ingredients onto the left side of your journal page; be sure to include any food items you have left over in your fridge. Name this column "Ingredients on Hand."

- *Step 2:* Look over the list of ingredients and star anything you're excited to try, foods you know you have recipes for, foods you want to research recipes for, and foods you want to eat first (perishable).

- *Step 3:* Spend a few minutes flipping through your favorite cookbook or browsing your favorite online cooking site. (Check out 101cookbooks .com by San Francisco–based Heidi Swanson for inspiration—you can search her amazing recipes by ingredients. Kris Carr also has some of my favorite recipes. But honestly, the entire Internet is your cookbook these days; you can find a recipe for anything just by typing it into Google. Your intuition is the best sous chef.) Find a few new meal ideas you can make throughout the week with what you have on hand.

- *Step 4:* Divide the meal ideas into categories under a "Meals I Have the Ingredients to Make" column: List them under "Breakfast," "Lunch," "Dinner," and "Snacks."

- *Step 5:* If there's anything additional you'll need, jot down those items on the right side of the page under an "Oops I forgot" column. Make yourself a note to grab these the next time you're out.

Meal Planner

Ingredients on Hand	Meals I Have the Ingredients to Make				Oops I forgot
	Breakfast	Lunch	Snacks	Dinner	

THE CLUTTER CLEARER

Detoxing our bodies gets all the hype—but what about detoxing our spaces? We spend so much time in our living spaces, and their state, of course, has a huge impact on our mental state. Clutter can create stagnation, so clearing it, embracing minimalism, and working with a capsule wardrobe (cutting my entire wardrobe down to less than 40 pieces) have drastically improved my health and happiness more than any other wellness practices I've tried (except journaling, of course!).

Creating change externally can spark internal change. That's why when I'm working with new clients, I usually encourage them to begin by creating space in their homes. If we want to make space for change, we must quite literally create room for it to come in. Personally, I don't allow myself to buy anything new without first giving something away. I constantly reassess all my belongings to determine what I can get rid of to live my most organized, minimal life. I used to be nostalgic for my belongings—especially clothing, thinking, *This might come back into style,* or *This might fit again eventually*—but then inspiration came to me from my feng shui master, friend, and podcast guest Anjie Cho (author of *108 Ways to Create Holistic Spaces*), which I've turned into two personal rules:

1. If I haven't worn a piece of clothing in a year, I have to give it away—regardless of its value or how much wear I got out of it.

2. With all other items, if I look at the item and it doesn't make me happy *in that exact moment,* then regardless of value, I get rid of it—or at the very least put it into storage. If it doesn't make me feel good, then why is it in my space?

The ideal resource for fully embracing this concept of clearing up your home as a precursor to clearing up your life is *The New York Times* best-selling book *The Life-Changing Magic of Tidying Up* by Marie Kondo. Kondo advises to clear clutter *as soon* and *as quickly* as possible, because every moment living in an untidy space is a moment not fully lived. I know what you're probably thinking . . . you just have so much to do and no time to fit in a major space detox. Let this tool be your guide to map out clutter clearing: schedule it, commit to it, make it fun, and get it done.

Directions:

- *Step 1:* **Assess your space.** Write down all the rooms in your living space, including closets and bathrooms.

- *Step 2:* **Rank your rooms.** Next, number each room in order of its importance to your well-being. So, think of the rooms that you spend the *most* time in; those will likely be highest on your list. Also consider the rooms that are most related to your personal goals. So, for example, if personal presentation is important to you, perhaps you rate your closet highest. If personal finance is most crucial, perhaps your office ranks number one. Or if your health is most pertinent, the kitchen will top your list. Ranking your rooms in this way will help you wrap your brain around what room to start with when tackling such a huge task—baby steps will comfort you and help you see progress.

- *Step 3:* **Get "moving."** Everyone knows that moving is a hassle; however, there's no better way to fully see how much you've accumulated over the years than by pulling things out from their nooks and crannies and packing it all up. Moving also gives you a deadline, forcing you to go through your things by a nonnegotiable date.

   So choose a hypothetical, nonnegotiable "move" date and put it in your calendar, and plan to complete your decluttering by then. Journal about what you can realistically commit to based on your lifestyle. Perhaps you can devote an entire weekend to speed clutter clearing, taking one room at a time, sprint style. Or perhaps you're more of a gradual cleaner and prefer to do one room over the course of a month, with a few devoted hours each weekend, slow and steady. Either way, you must draft your plan. Perhaps even share it with someone to enlist their help or simply to keep you accountable.

- *Step 4:* **Create a simple rule.** In Marie Kondo's breakthrough bestseller, she advises readers to ask themselves a simple question when assessing their belongings: *Does it spark joy?* If so, you keep it. If not, you toss it. Simple as that. So brainstorm in your journal about one simple rule you can use for assessing your items, one guideline you want to adhere to. For instance, maybe for your wardrobe your rule is, *Have I worn this in the past year?* Or, *Would I wear it tomorrow without a second thought?*

- *Step 5:* **Make it fun.** Your free time is precious, and if you don't make clutter clearing a pleasurable activity, you won't do it—period. So journal about some ways you can liven up the experience of decluttering. Perhaps you'll invite a friend over to drink champagne with you as you model the contents of the depths of your closet and decide what to give away, Carrie Bradshaw–style. Perhaps you'll choose a show on Netflix to binge watch on your laptop while you work on a particular room, or cue up some motivational music, podcasts, and audiobooks to accompany you through the process.

- *Step 6:* **Treat yourself.** No doubt, we're more likely to work harder if we're motivated by a reward. So as you're mapping out your master plan for decluttering your space (ranking your rooms, choosing your "move" date, crafting your simple rule, and thinking up ways to make it fun), include a motivating reward for after you complete each room, or even each round, in your clutter clearing. This can be anything from buying movie tickets for the evening, signing yourself up for your favorite yoga class, or making dinner reservations at your favorite restaurant. You can even use the money you make from selling some of your belongings that no longer serve you to fund your reward!

THE PRIORITIZER

As humans we feel "productive" simply by crossing anything off our list, so it's easy to get wrapped up in exclusively doing mundane day-to-day tasks, e-mails, and errands—expending so much of our willpower that we have nothing left for taking inspired action toward our big goals.

This tool was inspired by high-performance coach, author, and speaker Brendon Burchard, who advises mapping out your day prior to opening your computer, checking your phone, or responding to anything. I take it a step further and prefer to do this the night before. That way when I wake up in the morning, I know exactly where to focus my energy for the day and I don't have to expend any precious resources on planning.

Burchard is not alone when it comes to proactively, rather than reactively, structuring your day. Leo Babauta, author and blogger of Zen Habits, recommends tackling your most important tasks first thing in the morning. He calls these your MITs (Most Important Tasks): the things you must finish in order to feel accomplished by the end of the day. This tool ensures that you not only identify your MITs but that you also complete them early enough in the day to later on tackle the tasks that require less of your mental focus.

This tool may seem quite simple, but I've found that the simplest changes are the ticket to increased productivity. Keeping your mornings productive is the key to deciding to have a good day.

Directions:

- *Step 1:* Before you go to bed or first thing in the morning, write down your top three most important tasks for the day ahead: the three things that you *must* accomplish in order to deem the day a success at its end. Keep this list to things that can be accomplished during one day, and make sure it represents tasks that, combined, will make you feel both *productive* and *creatively fulfilled.* (Perhaps two of these priorities are related to work but one is in the direction of a personal goal you're working toward, therefore ensuring that you're not only productive but also creatively fulfilled.)

    Note: It's likely that at least one thing on your list will *not* be urgent and have a strict deadline—that's the point. These are the things that are important to you but often get put off or placed on the back burner by the seemingly urgent requests from others and mundane day-to-day admin tasks. By putting these important things at the top of your list, you'll ensure they'll actually get completed.

- *Step 2:* Draw a line and write out all your other tasks beneath the line: things that must get done but are not necessarily contributing to big (productive, creative) goals and don't require much effort. For example: "Pick up the dry cleaning," "Empty the dishwasher," "Make that phone call," "Respond to that e-mail," etc. The more you list, the more you get to cross off (and who doesn't love making check marks?).

  In this bottom portion, you can also list all the people you need to connect with that day, including who you need to reach out to or follow up with. This allows you to go into your inbox armed with intention, rather than pure reaction, and reach out to these people first before addressing any other mail.

- *Step 3:* Make a commitment that for each task you complete off the bottom half of your list, you *must* complete an item from the top part before moving on. This ensures the important tasks without strict deadlines still get completed—and early enough in the day—and sets you up to feel accomplished and proactive throughout your entire day.

PART III

LET IT OUT TO FIND PRESENCE

Enjoy the Moment All Day

"Life is available only in the present. That is why we should walk in such a way that every step can bring us to the here and now."
— THICH NHAT HANH

While not all of us are monks or meditation masters, we can bring more mindfulness into our busy lives. We can breathe deeply while we're chopping vegetables in the kitchen, be more present while engaging with a stranger, or even chant a mantra while we drive. Awareness is the key to any self-study practice, from yoga to tapping to meditation; becoming aware of both your physical body and mind in any moment is crucial to such modalities.

I realized recently how much I actually lacked presence. I was spending so much time living in my head, thinking, anticipating, and planning my next moment, that I was completely missing the moment I was in. My thoughts looked something like this: While eating dinner, between bites I'd be stressfully thinking, *What could I have for dessert? No, I shouldn't have dessert—or wait, should I? Maybe I'll be hungry. My meal was actually small. I deserve it; it's been a long week. No, wait until breakfast. Have a big breakfast; that's better. You should go to bed early so you can wake up early to make breakfast. Wait, what am I doing tomorrow? Oh! I need to be at the airport early; I won't have time for breakfast. Have the dessert now! No, it's too late. That would take time to digest, and I can't afford to sleep poorly. What time do I need to leave for the airport? I hope I'm not late. Did I remember to pack everything? I'm nervous about my trip . . .* The next thing I know, my dinner plate is clean, yet I don't remember eating dinner at all because my mind was elsewhere—I never even tasted my food.

Has something like this happened to you before? Perhaps you're so "in your head" driving home that you don't remember the drive, and the next thing you know, you're pulling into your driveway—but you don't even remember getting there.

I'm a planner by nature, so I was constantly planning and living for my future self . . . which in theory seems great, but in reality I was missing the moment I was in by planning for a future vision that might never come. I realized the key to happiness is in the present moment; happiness can exist only there. While excitement and anticipation are fun emotions, the present is where all the magic and action are happening—you don't want to miss it.

How do you cultivate this presence? The best way to become aware of your body is simply to return to your breath.

Noticing the rise and fall of your chest and feeling the air pass in and out of your nostrils will tune you back in to your body. From your feet to your hands, notice how the air feels around you, notice all the sounds of the room, and look around and quietly observe. Using your senses is the best way to return to your body and get present to the moment you're in.

But what about your mind? How do you become aware of what's going on in there and settle into a place of mental peace when you're on the go, out in public, and being pulled in a million directions?

One word: *write.*

The best way for me to tune in when I'm out of the moment is by writing down my feelings, and the tools in this section can go with you anywhere and be done at any time to do just that. Toss a pocket journal into your bag in case you need to turn to it on the go. I sometimes forget my portable journal—but what's one thing you have with you no matter where you go? Your phone! The best part of this tech-savvy selfie era is that we as a society always have this journal of sorts with us at all times.

Some of my most profound thoughts were written in my iPhone Notes app. One time I literally had to pull over while driving when I got a strong feeling that I should write a blog post; I wrote the entire thing on my iPhone—and to this day it is my most viewed post. There are many other great apps, like my favorites Evernote and Google Drive, which sync your notes so that they're accessible on any platform.

The point is, you don't need to be in a fancy meditation space to let it out. Frequently, a funky feeling that needs to be released will hit you while you're on a hike, at work, or running errands. I stop, drop, and journal whenever I feel the need. The techniques in this section can be done any time of day to tune you back in to your thoughts. So take a deep breath, exhale, and let it out to enjoy the moment.

- 14 The Joy Jar
- 15 The Repeat Thought List
- 16 The Meal Companion Worksheet
- 17 The Situation Step Back
- 18 The Way Out of Compare & Despair
- 19 Write Your Way Out of a Funk
- 20 The Make-Any-Situation-Fun Tool

TOOL NO. 14

THE JOY JAR

We so often rush through happy moments without even realizing our joy. Sure, the big wins of the day we remember, like getting a raise or finishing a major project. But it's the simple moments, which are often rushed through and forgotten, that consistently bring us the most joy . . . the parking attendant's smile, the taste of your tea, the yoga pose that you nailed. This tool will help you notice the joy occurring all around you in real time and document it simultaneously. When you become aware of joy in the present moment, you actively start to seek out more in your life.

While you can certainly jot down these moments in your journal, I like to take it a step further: fill a jar with moments of joy. Knowing that you've made a commitment to fill a jar to the brim with joy by the end of the year (or whatever period of time you choose) will require you to actively pursue it. This is a great exercise to involve others in: friends, partners, and even kids.

Don't worry if you forget to add some joy to the jar one day, because it will balance out on those amazing days where you add multiple pieces of joy. The beauty of the Joy Jar is that it's always there for you, depending on how you need it—you're either giving it joy, or it's giving joy back to you. This practice will dramatically increase the joy factor in your life not only because you're seeking out more joy, but because you're noticing, acknowledging, documenting, and then returning the joy that's occurring all around you.

Directions:

- *Step 1:* Grab a large empty mason jar. Feel free to decorate or label it as your Joy Jar. Keep it by your bed, by your front door, or somewhere you will see or pass by it daily.

- *Step 2:* Each day, write down one or more things that went well that day, or a moment when you felt joy. You can write these moments in your portable journal or on scraps of paper, or simply note them in your phone to write down later. This can be done throughout the day as these moments occur, or you can set a timer on your phone to go off twice a day (I like the idea of lunchtime and later in the evening)—and each time the alarm goes off, stop, drop, and jot.

- *Step 3:* When you get home, tear off that piece of paper and add it to the jar, or jot down your notes from your phone on a scrap of paper and put it in the jar.

- *Step 4:* Whenever you're feeling down, close your eyes and reach into the jar to grab a moment. Read it. Soak up its joy, and put it back.

- *Step 5:* On New Year's Eve, your birthday, or any day you deem special, open the jar and read all your joyous moments from the year. Be flooded with all of that goodness.

THE REPEAT THOUGHT LIST

We have over 60,000 thoughts a day. However, according to research, as many as 98 percent of these thoughts are the *same few thoughts* on repeat. And of those, 80 percent are negative.

The purpose of this tool is to acknowledge your thoughts and to identify patterns, noticing which thoughts are repeating, and then become more aware of them, both negative and positive—without judgment. Remember that all your thoughts with strong feelings behind them manifest in some form, good or bad, so keeping your thoughts positive is crucial to helping you create better feelings, and your good feelings in turn will help you create the life you desire.

The key to this exercise, though, is *not* to be hard on yourself. As *A Course in Miracles* says, don't judge your ego with your ego. Instead of being critical of yourself for negative, repetitive thoughts, look at them as powerful opportunities to pivot, and be grateful you're recognizing them. Use your feelings and emotions as indicators of where your thoughts are. If you're feeling good, chances are your *thoughts* are good, and therefore your physical experience will reflect your high-vibe internal situation back at you. This tool will help you get in the thick of your thoughts and change course, if needed, by shifting them.

Directions:

- *Step 1:* This tool doesn't need to be done every day, so choose just one day to use as a random sample for this experiment. Try to select a day where you won't mind interrupting yourself to make notes in your journal.

- *Step 2:* Set a timer on your phone to go off randomly, or every 10 or 15 minutes. Every time the timer goes off, stop what you're doing and write down the thoughts that were just on your mind. Don't judge the thoughts; just get them down.

- *Step 3:* At the end of the day, take stock of all the thoughts you've transcribed in your journal, and look for repeated thoughts or patterns. Circle or star the ones that appear on repeat.

- *Step 4:* Analyze these repeated thoughts without judgment. Just notice what they're trying to tell you. Try to backtrack to where some of these thoughts might have come from, and notice if their origin was actually false. For example, you might have thought on repeat: *I am ugly and unlovable.* However, looking back, you recognize the circumstances that could have contributed to that thought: *Actually, I grabbed the wrong pants and felt uncomfortable in my outfit all day. Or, I haven't been taking care of myself and giving myself the love I need since I've been so stressed.* Through this tool, you can begin to see how one negative thought changed the entire course of your day, and you can start to pivot out of it.

THE MEAL COMPANION WORKSHEET

We often eat fast, on the go, and sometimes without even realizing what we're eating. By nature I'm a fast eater and tend to scarf down my food in mere seconds—and if I'm distracted or scrolling through Instagram between bites, I won't even feel like I've eaten. My stomach might be bursting, yet my brain hasn't gotten the memo that I've had food, so I'm already thinking about what I can eat next . . . or feeling guilty about the amount I did eat without being present for it. That's why mindful eating is a powerful practice. It forces us to be aware of every sensation of our meals and how they're making us feel. By being more present for our meals, we'll feel more gratitude—and may even find our food more flavorful.

This tool is obviously not something to do every time you eat. You would not be much fun on a date or at a dinner if you whipped out this book and tried it each time. This tool is a way to check in with your body, and notice how your food is nourishing you emotionally and physically. It requires time and awareness. Practice it occasionally, while alone, to bring a level of mindfulness to your meal. The more you use it, the more presence and gratitude will naturally carry over into your other meals when you're around people, multitasking, or in a hurry.

Directions:

- *Step 1:* Just before eating, and with your meal in front of you, write down how you feel. For instance, perhaps you feel stressed, rushed, or unhappy and are using this meal as a way to relax, slow down, and make yourself happy. That's completely fine; just notice. Eating the meal might help you feel better. Or perhaps you're feeling happy, hungry, and calm. Any way you feel is fine; there's no right or wrong.

- *Step 2:* After you've reflected on how you feel, answer this question: How do you *want* to feel after completing this meal? Perhaps energized, light, fueled, and fed. Or maybe, depending on the meal, you want to feel deep pleasure, contentment, and joy.

- *Step 3:* Take a bite and put down your fork. Write down how you felt after that one bite. Do you want more? Was it as good as you were expecting? Just write it out. Then reflect: What are you grateful for about this moment?

- *Step 4:* Continue eating until your meal is half finished. Then put down your fork again and ask yourself these questions: *Am I still hungry? Am I full, but want to finish what's in front of me anyway? If so, why do I want to finish?* Just be aware, and honestly write how you're feeling.

- *Step 5:* When you've completed your meal, check in with yourself. Sit for a moment, and reflect on these questions: How do you feel now that it's over? Was the meal missing anything? What was the best part? Finally, how was your experience of the meal changed by reflecting on it throughout eating?

THE SITUATION STEP BACK

When a situation arises that stirs up your emotions, stop, drop, and *let it out*. This could be anything: a family member pushing your buttons, a boyfriend not calling you back, a snarky comment from a friend on social media, or a backhanded remark in an e-mail from your boss. These situations have the power to take us out of our flow. We replay them in our minds, and they not only majorly annoy us but also can hold us back for days—or even months if not dealt with.

Instinctive human reactions usually go one of two ways, depending on your personality type. You're either reactive, meaning you'll tend to defend yourself in the moment by being rude back, or you're submissive, meaning that you'll likely retreat and hold on to your anger and frustration long after the confrontation. Neither is a good solution.

The middle ground is to give yourself the needed time and space to take a step back from the situation, and this is the ultimate tool to let it out in the moment. It allows you both to feel your pain and to release it—literally by deleting it. By doing so, you send a sign to the Universe that you're ready to let it go. And if you need an extra boost, use a mantra from *A Course in Miracles*—"In my defenselessness my safety lies"—and give yourself time to step back from any distressing situation.

Directions:

- *Step 1:* **Become aware**. When a situation arises that makes you feel discomfort, hurt, or anger, simply notice that emotion in you. Before reacting to it or retreating to replay it in your mind, decide to *stop* and take a step back. If possible, physically remove yourself from the situation to gain some distance or space.

- *Step 2:* **"You oughta know . . ."** Once you've gained some distance (physical or mental) from the situation and have more clarity, write an e-mail directed to the person who stirred up the negative emotions in you—but leave the "To" line blank. Better yet, just write this in your on-the-go journal to prevent any accidental sending; however, treat it like it's a real e-mail. Go ahead and write out everything you're feeling about the situation—really get all your anger out (pretend you're Alanis Morissette singing "You Oughta Know"). Be sure to include how the other person hurt you, how it made you feel, why it was wrong, and how he or she could have been better. Now put the e-mail or note aside.

- *Step 3:* **Return to it**. Read the note later in the day, or better yet the next morning or even a few days after the incident when you've had time to cool down from the initial burn. On this fresh read, put yourself in the other person's shoes. Why might they have treated you this way? Was it really about you, or could they have something else going on? Then look more objectively at your side of the street. What was your part in the situation? Is there anything within you that allowed the other person to do this to you?

- *Step 4:* **End it.** End the note—and with it, any resentment you're still holding on to—with how you would have preferred the other person handle the situation. Then check in with how you feel now. Has the feeling lessened? Released?

Finally, do yourself the ultimate loving favor: forgive, forget, and—of course—delete.

THE WAY OUT OF COMPARE & DESPAIR:

"Concern Yourself with You"

When I was a kid, my mom would constantly tell me something that sticks with me to this day. It became a mantra I used in elementary school, carried on to high school, and still use today well into adulthood. When I found myself constantly making choices based on other kids, my mom would say to me, "Concern yourself with you."

Comparison is an easy trap to get caught in. With the advent of social media long after my mom first uttered the epic "Concern yourself with you" mantra, I wonder if perhaps she was predicting what was to come in an era where comparing yourself to other peoples' highlight reels is easier and more addictive than ever.

Have you ever gone on a social stalking binge of someone, and next thing you know you're so far down their Instagram feed that your thumbs hurt from scrolling and you pray they won't slip and accidently double-tap a photo, "liking" it and revealing how deep into their past you've scrolled? (Um, yeah . . . clearly that's too specific to not be an autobiographical example.) Anyway, after talking with countless people I realized I wasn't alone, and this comparison game is rampant. I found myself giving the same advice to my friends and clients that my mom gave me long ago.

This tool guides us to take my mom's advice and quit the compare-and-despair game we so often default to. Whether it's a mentor, a guru, a celebrity, your accomplished friend from high school, or your ex-boyfriend's new girlfriend, comparing yourself keeps you stuck and makes you feel less than.

Conan O'Brien once said in a commencement speech at Dartmouth that comedians of his generation desperately wanted to be the next David Letterman. He remarked, "It is our failure to become our perceived ideal that ultimately defines us and makes us unique." I found that to be a deeply profound lesson of authenticity. We have to concern ourselves with our own truth, and not try to emulate anyone else's.

The bottom line is that whenever you're comparing yourself to others, you're not concerned with you. The interesting thing is, the more you are *yourself,* the more attractive you become. This tool guides you to instead use who you're comparing yourself to as a guide for something you want more of within yourself, which probably isn't being fully expressed.

Directions:

- *Step 1:* Make a list of the people you most compare yourself to. Then examine how you're separating yourself by answering these two questions for each person on your list (if there are several people, choose just one or two for this exercise today):

a) *Are you making yourself "more special" or "better" than those you are comparing yourself to? If yes, move on to Step 2.*

b) *Are you making yourself "less special" or "worse" than those you're comparing yourself to? That is, are you regarding <u>them</u> as better than you or more special by either idolizing them or feeling jealousy toward them? If yes, move on to Step 3.*

- *Step 2:* Answer the following questions in your journal if you answered "yes" to question (a) above:

  - *What is it within you that feels insecurity around this person you're comparing yourself to?*

  - *What is it within you that makes you feel like you need to perceive yourself as better than him or her?*

  - *In what ways are you both equal?*

  - *How can you see him or her with love instead?*

  When you're done, move on to Step 4.

- *Step 3:* Answer the following questions in your journal if you answered "yes" to question (b) above:

  - *What are the specific qualities or attributes that you find most inspiring about this person you're comparing yourself to?*

- *What is he or she mirroring back to you regarding qualities that are within you but are perhaps unawakened?*

- *How can you look at him or her as a positive example of inspiration?*

- *How can you embrace ways you are unique from him or her and love those qualities about yourself?*

- *In what ways are you both equal?*

- *Can you find common humanity with him or her?*

- *Step 4:* Now concern yourself with you. Write a sentence about yourself in the third person as if *someone else* were admiring *you.* This is your time to toot your own horn, which may feel uncomfortable. It does for me, but I'll take one for the team and give you an example: "Katie is an awesome podcast host, really kills it on the ukulele, knows how to write a mean journal prompt, and has an adorable little dog." See there, that wasn't so bad—give it a go!

- *Bonus step:* Tweet your 140-character horn toot at me (@katiedalebout)! I want to see how awesome you are.

WRITE YOUR WAY OUT OF A FUNK

"If you're feeling helpless, help someone." Burmese activist Aung San Suu Kyi hits the nail on the head with that line, and it's the inspiration for this tool. This is an extremely powerful exercise that helps you feel better by figuring out how you can help someone else. You may be thinking, *How will helping others change my funky state of being?* It seems counterintuitive, but it's the way the Universe works. We're hardwired to feel good by helping others. The Universe is so crafty, isn't it? It made it so that being helpful feels really awesome, therefore making us want to do it, therefore making the world awesome.

I guarantee that this tool will radically shift your energy immediately. However, make sure your efforts are genuine and backed with love—not "Oh, if I do this for you, then that tool from my journal book will work, and I'll feel better because that happy girl told me to . . ." Nope. Helping purely to people-please doesn't work either; that type of "helpfulness" will not only keep you stuck in your funk but will probably pull you in deeper like quicksand! Just help, while expecting nothing in return.

Directions:

- *Step 1:* Whenever you feel off, out of sorts, or in a funk, grab your journal and list five ways you can be of service, or five people you can help. It can be anything from raking leaves for your elderly neighbor to calling your friend who just went through a breakup and lending an ear.

- *Step 2:* Write down a commitment to yourself to take action immediately on at least one of the five ways you listed. And next time you need a jolt of helpfulness, consult the list, take action on one of the items, and replace it with a new idea.

THE MAKE-ANY-SITUATION-FUN TOOL

In any given situation, it's your responsibility to make it fun. If you're driving or cleaning, make sure that you have a good podcast or soundtrack on; if you're working on your finances, then have your favorite drink in hand, a nice outfit on, and a comfortable chair to sit in. You can make mundane things, and even things you dread, fun by simply slowing down and planning in a bit of pleasure.

I love this tool because it arms you to go into every situation with mindfulness—especially those situations that you'd usually dread and rush through. Oprah once said that when she makes her bed (which she says she only does on weekends), she pretends that she's Martha Stewart by getting into it with the throw pillows and really fluffing them. This insight, believe it or not, deeply changed me, because I realized that pretending you're a professional at whatever you're doing makes it immediately more entertaining. The most mundane tasks or situations don't stand a chance with this tool in your repertoire.

Directions:

- *Step 1:* **Describe what you're dreading.** Maybe it's meeting with your new boss or your in-laws, attending a work conference, cleaning your bathroom, wiping the snow off your car, or even going to a funeral. Describe the situation in your journal in vivid detail, including what it will be like, who will be there, and most important, how you feel about it.

- *Step 2:* **Add some pleasure.** With the situation in mind, ask yourself what would make it even a bit more pleasurable. For instance, while you clear snow off your car, could you put your headphones in with your favorite podcast and bundle up? While you meet with your new boss, could you bring an essential oil that you love, keeping something that calms you in your bag? Could you listen to music while you clean? Could you drink your favorite tea while at the work conference? Could you wear your favorite shoes to meet your in-laws? Just start writing down all the ways that you could plan to make the situation better.

- *Step 3:* **Game on.** After you've decided how to add some pleasure, start to think in a big-picture way and ask yourself how you could make the situation a game. Can you start to count all the blue things you see while you're stuck in a long line? Can you time yourself and see if you can clear your car of snow before a song ends? Can you pretend you're a professional therapist as you comfort someone having a tough time? Instead of judging an experience as negative or mundane, look at it as a challenge to figure out how you can make it into a fun game. Keep in mind that any situation is more fun when you're being of service and being helpful. You're more powerful than you think when it comes to creating a situation that's pleasurable.

PART IV

LET IT OUT TO CREATE ABUNDANCE

Making Space for Manifesting

"Be thankful for what you have; you'll end up having more. If you concentrate on what you don't have, you will never, ever have enough."
— OPRAH WINFREY

Abundance doesn't just mean money. It encompasses all the things we value, including our time, relationships, and lifestyle. We each have our own story when it comes to these things—the common thread, though, is that our long-ago-formed beliefs about abundance impact our lives *now*. To become more abundant, I had to shift to *thinking*, and the tools in this section are what I used to change my mind-set from a lack mentality to an abundant one.

But first let's take a step back and touch upon the aspect of money for a minute, since it's such a pervasive part of life. Sometimes we don't want to look at our financial life . . . as if somehow it will just sort itself out. That was the case for me. I worked through college but had significant help from my parents while I was in school, so I assumed (much like Hannah Horvath on HBO's *Girls*) that this financial support would just continue after graduation if I worked only part-time teaching yoga and bounced around in unpaid internships.

Oh man, even writing that sentence feels awful—not just because it makes me sound entitled and unmotivated, but because it's uncomfortable and embarrassing to remember how epically clueless I was when it came to how to support myself. In school we're taught geometry—so we can craft the perfect shot in mini golf?—yet we never learn how to manage our money? It often becomes something we end up learning on our own, often the hard way.

As I mentioned earlier, out of college I got a full-time job so I'd be able to fully support myself. I resisted at first because all I wanted to do at the time was blog and teach yoga, two things I still love to do but—I quickly realized—would not yet pay the bills or afford me the luxury of living on my own, which I desperately wanted. So I took that full-time job and immersed myself in a career, even though my heart was with my creative passions: blogging, yoga, and writing, which were all lacking as a result of my new time-consuming job. I knew I needed to get back into them, but I wasn't willing to give up my independence and knew I couldn't support myself with my creative pursuits alone. I felt completely stuck.

This changed with a prayer.

A prayer is simply an intention or a request. Many of us, myself included prior to this realization, tend to be SOS pray-ers—meaning we only pray when something has veered extremely off track and we have no other option than to cry out for help to something bigger than ourselves. That's one way of praying. However, if you want to create real abundance in your life, pray when things go right *and* wrong, pray with gratitude, and pray often. (Think of the Universe as a friend. If you call that friend only when you need something, that would be pretty annoying.) My prayer was:

> *Dear Universe,*
>
> *Thank you for this financially supporting work. Please make it fun and calm, and use my natural talents and capabilities for good. Thank you for giving me awesome people to work with and opportunities for learning through my work. I ask to be in even deeper gratitude for the money it gives me, and I ask that it energize me so I can do the creative work I desire that serves the highest good most. Thanks so much for guiding me.*
>
> *~ Katie*

This prayer was transformative because it shifted my perception about my career. I stopped looking at my full-time job as a roadblock to where I wanted to go but rather saw it as a *doorway into it*. Ironically, during the busiest season of my job I had more growth in my side hustle blogging, coaching, and writing career than when I was living at home and exclusively blogging. Since I knew I was busy, I got organized,

I managed my time well, and I cut out all procrastination. You actually get more done when you're busy. I had manifested exactly what I wanted, and abundance and goodness started flowing into my life. Why was that?

The beauty of this situation was that my blog and podcast grew so organically because I no longer had any intention of monetizing them; rather, I focused solely on giving free content and value while asking nothing in return from my audience. I was able to do this because my full-time job supported my needs; I didn't *need* to make money from my blog and podcast. This put me in a groovy position where I didn't need advertisers or to actively seek coaching clients to mentor; I simply allowed the ideal people to reach out to me when they were ready. I shared solely for the love of it and got even more love back.

Through these experiences, I learned three crucial keys for creating abundance and making space for manifesting it into our lives:

Think abundantly. The more you say "I can't afford that" or "I don't have the time" (or any limiting statements like that), the more that will be true. Instead say, "I'm choosing not to buy that" or "I'm choosing to spend my time this way," and remember that every time you reframe your thoughts, your future self will thank you.

Believe you are worthy. Raising your self-worth is key. If you don't believe you're worthy of abundance, the Universe won't give you that prosperity because there's a part of you that doesn't believe you deserve it. The more you believe in your worth and what you have to give to the world, the more resources you will manifest to be able to do that. You must become an energetic match to abundance and prosperity to physically receive it.

Give freely. The more you give, the more you receive. As a kid I would always watch my mom and aunt fight over who would get the bill at restaurants, each of them wanting to treat the other. Whether they knew it or not, they were teaching me the concept that what you give is exactly what you get. While neither of them expected anything in return, there was an unconscious knowing that eventually it would all even out—they were simply exchanging value.

Watching this for years, it has become part of me. When I'm at dinner with friends, I always just pick up the bill. Not because I'm rolling in the dough. In fact many times it's been quite the opposite, and my bank account was pretty empty. But I still treated because it was a lunch. I wasn't buying them a car; I was likely buying a veggie burger, and treating them was worth every penny to me. I felt abundant being able to do something nice for a friend, and I think of it as paying for the experience—the conversation and the love. And after a while when I was struggling to buy meals and everyone wanted to treat me, I felt like my mom and aunt, fighting for the bill and losing every time.

That's what happens when you give freely without expectation of receiving anything in return—eventually you do. Give value and it will come back to you always, like a straight-up boomerang. Trust me.

- 21 The HappyThankYouMorePlease Tool
- 22 Texts from Yourself
- 23 The Job Love Letter

TOOL NO. 21

THE HAPPYTHANKYOU MOREPLEASE TOOL

Have you ever had a really great feeling come over you out of nowhere, and you just want to stay there . . . but all too soon reality takes over and so it only lasts a brief moment? What if the next time a moment like that happened, you could stay in it a little longer? Perhaps it's a nostalgic memory triggered by hearing a song or smelling a scent, or it's a moment of presence and happiness while you're on the beach with your favorite people—regardless of what it is, you want to prolong it, even linger there forever.

What if I told you that you could?

That's what this tool is all about: getting you to (a) notice you're in this blissed-out moment through awareness, (b) find some gratitude for that, and (c) ask for more from the Universe.

There were a wide range of things that inspired the tools in this book, and *this* one was inspired by one of my favorite movies, *Happythankyoumoreplease* by Josh Radnor, who wrote, directed, and starred in it. There's this beautiful monologue in the film where a cabdriver advises his passenger, the character Annie, that bliss is her birthright, that the key to happiness is gratitude, and that she need only have more gratitude to be happy. When Annie asks how he suggests she do this, the cabdriver says it's simple. He tells her to say thank you. And then say more please.

Not only is this the title of the movie; it's my favorite lesson because what he's saying to her—at least in my interpretation—is basically each time you notice an awesome moment, say in your mind *Thank you,* and then say in your mind *More please* as a way of sending a signal to the Universe that you'll have more of that awesome feeling . . . please. It's essentially a prayer, a request, and a desire, and by claiming it you're not only more likely to receive it but also to notice and appreciate it when you do.

Honestly, if you do these steps, you'll notice after a while the Universe becomes a lot like Jimmy John's, delivering your orders *"so fast you'll freak."*

Directions:

- *Step 1:* For this tool you'll want to write in something you likely have with you all the time—your phone. Create a note in your smartphone called "HappyThankYouMorePlease . . ." This will be a running note.

- *Step 2:* As you're out and about throughout your day, each time a good feeling washes over you, whip out your phone and complete this sentence:

  "Thank you for _____
  _____; more please."

- *Step 3:* Put your phone away and return to enjoying the moment you're in. You've cultivated some gratitude, you've gotten present, and you've sent your desire order straight to the Universe.

TEXTS FROM YOURSELF

Most of us have the Golden Rule reversed; we tend to treat others *far* better than we treat ourselves. For instance, think of how nice we are to our friends, and then compare that with some of the self-talk that goes on in our heads. The way we tend to talk to ourselves is extremely negative. We would likely be appalled if the mean thoughts we think about ourselves were broadcast for all to see: harsh criticisms about our bodies, nasty comparisons to others, rude remarks about not feeling good or smart enough. Contrary to what many might believe, self-criticism will *not* help us change in any way—it's unproductive. You can't hate yourself and expect love. You can't shame yourself to acceptance.

By checking in daily, or perhaps even hourly, with ourselves in a gentle way with this tool, we're retraining our mind to be loving in order to attract more positivity, wellness, and abundance into our lives. And the more we do this, the more we raise the energy of the world.

Treating yourself as well as you treat your friends seems simple, but it will have a dramatic effect on your happiness and well-being. Think about it: "Treat others how you want to be treated" only works if you're treating *yourself* with kindness first.

Directions:

- *Step 1:* Set a reminder on your phone to go off once a day, or perhaps choose a day out of the week and set a reminder to go off every hour. This reminder should say: *Hey, how are you? How are you feeling?* (just as you would check in with a friend you haven't talked to in a while).

- *Step 2:* When your phone alert chimes with these questions, return to the present and take out your journal. Take inventory of how you're feeling, and respond to your self-check-in by answering those questions.

- *Step 3:* After you ask yourself how you're feeling, now take inventory of what you need. Ask yourself, *What do you need to feel better?* For instance, perhaps you catch yourself stuck in money fears. In that case, use this as an opportunity to befriend and nurture yourself by asking, *What's something nice I can treat you to today?* Treating yourself doesn't have to be expensive; it can be as simple as going on a walk, listening to your favorite podcast, or playing your favorite song.

THE JOB LOVE LETTER

Whether you adore your current career or are manifesting new employment, this tool can transform any work situation for the better. You'll get clear on what's working for you and what's not in your job, which will help you articulate your feelings to your boss, co-workers, and even prospective employers. Once you gain some clarity, you'll then look at what you're grateful for about your position. Gratitude is key in any situation; by focusing on the good, you'll create more of it in your current or new (soon-to-manifest!) environment.

Remember that, especially in our careers, there's a plan far greater than ours, and how we envision our ideal career or job could be just a *fraction* of what is possible for us. The job you desire might be modest compared to the career the Universe is creating for you—maybe in a company that doesn't even yet exist—but you block yourself from receiving that abundance when you're too fixated on your original path.

So stay open, and remember that the best way to receive a promotion, a new client, or a great work opportunity is to be the best that you can be in your current role, going above and beyond, showing up fully, and finding all you can to enjoy about it. Trust that with clarity and gratitude, you *will* be supported.

Directions:

- *Step 1:* Open to a fresh blank page in your journal and address it to your current job: it can be to a specific person—such as your boss, a co-worker, or a client—or you can even write to the job as a whole. I've done this exercise multiple times and prefer writing to my job as a whole (not the company, but the entire work situation, including roles and responsibilities).

- *Step 2:* In your letter, start by stating exactly how you're feeling: about the position, the pay, your performance, the support of your boss or your team, and so on. Get clear, and get it all out and down on paper.

- *Step 3:* In the next paragraph, focus solely on what you *love* and *are grateful for* concerning the position. Perhaps your list is a mile long, or maybe you struggle to get anything out at all. I'm confident that if you dig deep, though, there are things about your job that you do love and appreciate, even if you're looking for a new one. Maybe you really love your ergonomic desk chair, or the water in the watercooler really hits the spot.

- *Step 4:* Sign off with "Love," and your name. Remember, this is a job love letter—so no better way to end it than with good vibes.

THE BECOMING IRRESISTIBLE TOOL

When you're living in true joy, you will be irresistible to everyone—including your ideal mate, current partner, or even just a person who wants to buy you a coffee. Therefore, happiness can't come *after* you have the perfect relationship; before you can attract love to your life, you must find complete happiness and love in your *own* life. If you want to feel deep intimacy in your current relationships, cultivating internal joy has to be the first step.

The second step to irresistibility is getting in touch with your feminine or masculine energy. The fiery passion that we crave in relationships is born out of the polarity of feminine and masculine, something that has nothing to do with gender. So once you've got joy down, focusing on amping up your femininity will attract the masculine partner you crave, and vice versa.

If you want to attract the best person for you, if you want to cultivate community in your life, or if you want to make your current relationships more intimate, this is the tool you've been waiting for—trust me.

Directions:

- *Step 1:* Create a list of what *happiness* and *joy* look like to you. What does it mean to be *fully alive*? What does it feel like, and how would you live from that place? Get specific, and narrow it down to your top three qualities that embody happiness and joy. For instance, perhaps it means smiling at everyone you pass by, hugging people that you meet rather than shaking hands, and making eye contact instead of phone contact in your conversations. Your list will be unique to you.

- *Step 2:* If you're working to attract a masculine partner, create a list of what embodying feminine energy looks like to you. If you're working to attract a feminine partner, create a list of what embodying masculine energy looks like to you. Narrow your list down to three specific virtues, ideals, or qualities that would enhance your femininity or masculinity, depending on whom you're seeking. With feminine energy, think creativity, openness, receptiveness, compassion, connection, nurture, and intuition. And with masculine energy, think strength, action, focus, movement, responsibility, generosity, clarity, and encouragement.

- *Step 3:* Check in with your two lists every day to make sure you're getting yourself into the deep space of irresistibility. Each morning as you look them over, visualize and decide how you will embody both the qualities of joy and either femininity or masculinity in your day ahead. The actions can be as simple as wearing a dress for femininity or jumping on your rebounder for joy.

THE IDEAL EXPERIENCE PLAY-BY-PLAY

Whether it's a family gathering that you're dreading, a job interview that's got you wound up, a vacation that you've been looking forward to for weeks, or even a morning where you feel a bit unsettled about the day ahead, committing to this exercise beforehand opens you up to the ideal situation occurring. This tool guides you to create a crystal clear vision of how you want to *feel* in any given event—which will give you the best chance to actually experience it when the situation arises.

There's one caveat, though. While you may write down your best possible scenario in great detail, it's important to not become attached to it. If we cling too tightly to our "ideal," we could block ourselves from even greater possibilities. As I've said before, our ideal might be only a *fraction* of what's actually possible for us, as the Universe may have better, bigger plans in store. So hold your vision loosely as an option of what's possible, and if things seem to be heading in the opposite direction of what you envisioned, remember: That new direction could be a sign that you're being led to something better than you even imagined.

Directions:

- *Step 1:* Prior to any event, whether it's something you're looking forward to or massively dreading, sit in stillness for 90 seconds and think about how you'd ideally like the experience to go. Just visualize.

- *Step 2:* Now grab your journal and write out what it *felt like* when you visualized the experience as everything you wanted it to be. Focus only on how you felt: Comfortable? Confident? Energized? Relaxed? Remember, in any situation you can *only* control your attitude and perspective, so focus solely on you here.

- *Step 3:* Now, take more time and play out every detail of the experience in your mind. Get super specific and clear, and detail the entire scenario and how you'd like it to go. This is the time to invite people and dialogue into your visualization. Who is around you? What is around you? What does it smell like? What is said? How do you handle yourself?

- *Step 4:* Finally, fast-forward to the end of the event and tune in to how you want to feel right after. Then ask yourself, how would you like to remember the experience, looking back weeks later?

TOOL NO. 26

THE MONEY MANIFESTER

Based off the work of Kate Northrup, the author of *Money: A Love Story* (a great resource for diving fully into this subject), this tool is a bit more complicated than some of the others in this book—but it's so worth it. I had Kate on my podcast, and her insights on money completely blew my mind. I recommend focusing on this tool solely for at least a week, if not longer, giving special attention to each step. It will help you release all that's blocking you from attracting abundance into your life and shift your focus from any neediness around money to renewed excitement about it.

If you can find ways to feel abundant now, you'll give off less lack and fear and get in a state of receptivity where you can attract more abundance into your life. The feeling of "need" breeds only more lack and fear, and abundance attracts abundance. The goal of this tool isn't for you to manifest tons of money right away (although that may be a by-product, certainly); it's first for you to *feel* more abundant in your current situation, which will help you become a match to receive that abundance. This works for everything in life, actually.

Yes, money is a deeply personal part of life, and our relationships with it can be complicated owing to our beliefs around it. However, money *itself* is simple. As Kate says, money is something humans made up as a stand-in for what we value. This tool guides you to uncomplicate your money relationship one step at a time; so go slow and let the cash flow.

Directions:

- *Step 1:* **Define your personal story regarding money.** Freewrite for at least 15 minutes on how you regard money, addressing your feelings about and beliefs around it both as you grew up and now in the present. Some questions to start you off:

  - *What was your experience with money as a child?*

  - *Were there any common sayings or concerns about money that your parents or other adults around you had?*

  - *What emotions do you associate with money now?*

  - *What excites you about money?*

  - *What frustrates you about money?*

  For example, maybe money was abundant for you as a child but your parents were never around and constantly working; they always told you that you have to work hard for your money. So you grew up associating having money with working hard and lacking any free time.

- *Step 2:* **Name one thing you haven't done because of money, and why.** Freewrite for at least 10 minutes on something you've held back doing because of money. For example, maybe you want to quit your full-time job to start your own business from home, or maybe you want to travel more or even move to a new country, but you believe the only way to have money is to work hard in a career you may not be completely happy in, or you may believe that you have to sacrifice your lifestyle for security. Let out whatever comes up for you.

- *Step 3:* **Reflect on your desire.** Read over what you wrote in Step 2, and shift your focus to why you want that one thing. Focusing on why you *can't* do it or *haven't* done it only clouds the reason you *wanted* to do it in the first place, so get back to this place of desire. Think of the best-case scenario rather than the worst, which is where our minds often jump to first, and examine why you want it—not all the reasons you're afraid or feel held back. These questions should get you started:

  - *Why do you want it?*
  - *What does doing it make possible for you?*
  - *What are some positive results of doing this?*
  - *How does it affect the people around you?*

- *Who will support you and be most excited about your choice?*

- *How will it make you feel happier?*

- *Step 4:* **Shift your focus to excitement.** Now, pretend you're doing this one thing *tomorrow,* and let all your feelings flow out onto the page. Focus on the excitement you'd feel if that opportunity were here. Then freewrite on the following questions:

  - *What would you do if money were no object?*

  - *How would you live?*

  - *What would you give?*

  - *Where would you travel?*

  - *What would you wear?*

- *Step 5:* **Ask yourself how you can live that way now.** Look over your work from Steps 3 and 4, start a fresh page, and with your renewed desire and excitement, journal about how you can live that way *now* with the money you do have. Perhaps you don't take the *Eat Pray Love*-esque adventure you wrote about, but you can go on a weekend away with a friend. Or perhaps you don't purchase an entire new wardrobe, but you swap some old items in your closet for some updated ones that make you feel like a million bucks.

Whatever ways you can find to *feel* abundant now, go for it. By pulling away from lack and fear and instead discovering ways to feel more abundant in your current situation, you'll be able to attract more abundance into your life because you'll become a match to receive it.

TOOL NO. 27

THE GRATITUDE ENHANCER

Gratitude is powerful—but you've probably heard that a million times before. From your uncle at Thanksgiving to Oprah on TV, everyone is telling us to be thankful. For a long time I didn't understand the power of gratitude, until I made a practice of it . . . and I kid you not, everything changed.

By focusing on what you have, you create more of what you want. This tool guides you not only to keep your gratitude focused on the day at hand but also to switch it up on the regular because, while thanking the Universe is powerful in all forms, simply saying thank you for your mom, your dog, or your car every day sometimes becomes more of a habit than a powerful practice. For gratitude to really work well, it's the feeling *behind* the words that matters most.

On some days you may struggle to begin your list, but once you write down even one item, you'll be surprised by how much gratitude pours out. Gratitude multiplies like bunnies. When you start to appreciate an area where your life is already abundant, eventually you'll see other areas becoming more abundant, too.

This tool is a smorgasbord of every gratitude practice I do on the regular. I hope you try them all out to decide which one speaks to you most, and continue with that technique consistently. Or you can become a gratitude ninja and work them all. Regardless, you have them in your repertoire now to use as you wish.

Directions:

Gratitude Practice #1—Thanksgiving Dinner for Your Mind

- *Step 1:* Keep a journal dedicated especially to this tool. I keep mine by my bed and try to write in it right before bed or first thing in the morning, so I won't forget. Each day, simply date the page and write down 5 to 10 things you're grateful for *that day.*

- *Step 2:* Every Thanksgiving, take time to yourself in order to review your year of gratitude. Look at the dates and notice who and what you were grateful for each day, as well as how your year changed and evolved based on what was going on in your life.

- *Step 3:* Begin a fresh journal each year to continue collecting gratitude.

Gratitude Practice #2—Deep Feeling Gratitude

- *Step 1:* Every so often I like to take one item from my long laundry list of gratitude and get down to the specifics of the feeling that piece of gratitude evokes in me. So, choose one item from your list of things you're grateful for.

- *Step 2:* Write in vivid detail about this one thing and how it makes you feel. By getting deeply involved in the emotion behind the thing you're grateful for, you allow even deeper gratitude to pour over you. (I learned this technique from Marie Forleo in one of her awesome weekly videos. She gave the vivid example of all the ways she's grateful for her fiancé, from how he makes the best pancakes to how he supports her in every way. Her talk was so filled with emotion it brought her to tears in the video, and me to tears watching it. It really depicted the level of emotion that deep gratitude can evoke in you.)

Gratitude Practice #3—Gratitude Group

- *Step 1:* Choose a few friends wanting to amp up the gratefulness in their lives. Perhaps it's other people on this *Let It Out* journey with you—or join the *Let It Out* Facebook crew and we'll link you up!

- *Step 2:* Start a chat using the WhatsApp app on your phone. (You could simply e-mail or text, but I find creating a separate chat through WhatsApp is highly effective because it's separate from all the other noise in our lives where it could easily get lost in the shuffle. Also, WhatsApp is completely free and allows you to text internationally, which is a bonus for me since my gratitude crew is around the world.)

- *Step 3:* Each day, send your crew a text with three things you're grateful for from that day. It's crucial that they're different every day, and that this group setting provides accountability for that. Try to limit your crew to no more than three, so that way you're not bombarded by texts all day long and you can actually read what your crewmates are sending, be happy for them, remind yourself to notice the moments of gratitude in your own day, and get inspired by what they're manifesting to step up your own manifesting game.

Gratitude Practice #4—Value Added Creates Value Added

- *Step 1:* Every day, jot down three (or more) ways you contributed to the world and are proud of yourself for that day. It could be as simple as helping a co-worker, calling your grandpa, or holding the door for someone.

- *Step 2:* Then think of a few ways other people helped you today. Perhaps someone then held the door for you, a friend sent you a text of encouragement, or your boyfriend took out your trash. Notice the exchange of value that occurs. The more we give, the more we receive; it's how the Universe is wired.

Gratitude Practice #5—Snap Stories of Gratitude

I'm no stranger to social media. I've loved Facebook since high school and wanted to upgrade my pink Razr flip phone to an iPhone purely for the purpose of having my own Instagram and not having to hack my boyfriend's phone to toss a Rise filter over photos of my salads. But when the social media app Snapchat came onto my radar, I resisted. It seemed overly complicated and, honestly, like a scary space full of naked photos that I had no desire to join. This all changed on a vacation when my friend Alex, a technology guru, busted out her selfie stick and taught me how to use Snapchat like a live gratitude journal.

- *Step 1:* The concept is simple. If you don't already have it, download the Snapchat app to your phone. Each day, starting in the morning, capture photos or 15-second video clips in Snapchat that are interesting, funny, beautiful, or happy moments of your day, and add them to your "Story." This shares them with your followers or friends, depending on your privacy settings.

- *Step 2:* At the end of each day, watch your story. It's crucial you do this every day because the beauty of Snapchat is that it autodeletes your story additions 24 hours after you post them. At the end of the day when I'm watching my story for that day, I feel so much gratitude for all the moments I noticed and captured throughout.

    If the day was particularly good, then I'll save my story, and if not, I'll just let it go, but taking that moment to visually watch the beauty of my day grounds me in the fact that *there is good in every day* no matter what—and at the same time, knowing Snapchat is right in my pocket reminds me to actively seek it out. If I stay in the house all day, my Snapchat isn't too interesting, so that encourages me not only to get out more but to see the world through a grateful lens when I do.

THE NEW MOON MANIFESTO

Manifestation is strongest within the first eight hours immediately following the new moon. Pretty neat, right? This is the prime time to focus your attention with great clarity on what you want to manifest, create, or bring into your life. This tool harnesses the power of the new moon and boosts your manifesting abilities to a whole new level.

If you think you have no experience with manifesting, you definitely do. As the Abraham-Hicks material teaches, our thoughts are *always* manifesting, but we're usually unconscious of it so we end up creating a reality with all sorts of things we didn't actually want! Most of us are visualizing negative outcomes all day long on repeat—we just call it "worrying"—and the more we worry, the more we attract things to worry about.

We're often so clear on what we don't want, we know exactly what that feels like. For instance, we don't want to be alone, but we know what loneliness feels like . . . and so that intention is reflected back to us. When it comes to what we do want, however, such as being in a loving, romantic relationship, that feeling might be foreign to us.

By stepping into the feelings that you want to become your new reality, you can create it. Trusting in the Universe is key, but so is realizing the part *you* play in the creation of your desire. As author and speaker Mastin Kipp says, just because you put something on your vision board—or vision page, in our case—doesn't mean you automatically deserve it. You must get yourself into alignment with what you desire before it can manifest off the page of your journal and into your life. You have to be able to *feel* what having it would be like before you actually have it physically. This takes focus and clarity, and this tool will help you become a match for what you're wanting before you can see it.

While this exercise is good to practice at any time of the year, manifestation is strongest during the new moon, and not a second before—so if the new moon is at 2:00 A.M., 1:59 A.M. is too early.

Directions:

- *Step 1:* For the strongest manifesting powers, wait until the new moon occurs in order to write out your desires. When the time is upon you, open your journal and create a wish list for what you want to manifest. Write down all your hopes, wishes, and desires. You can even add in visuals, creating a mobile vision board right in your journal by printing photos or cutting out magazine images. Focus on how you want to *feel* with what it is that you want to manifest.

- *Step 2:* Look over what you've written, and if there's anything on your list that doesn't make you come alive and completely excite you, cross it out and replace it immediately. It's important to get down to the nitty-gritty of how all these things make you feel, and keep only the ones that overwhelm you with good emotion.

- *Step 3:* Stare at your vision page for one minute, absorbing everything you've written down and really feeling the words. On the next page, freewrite for at least five minutes on the type of person you would need to be in order to have all the things and feelings that you described come into form. Let your pen flow, and don't hold back.

- *Step 4:* Once you've laid it all out on the page, forget about it. Completely let it go, trusting that the Universe will take care of it and bring it all to you in the perfect time and form. You can flip open to these pages in your journal anytime you need a jolt of inspiration.

THE COOLEST TOOL IN THE BOOK

Goals seem more real as soon as you write them down, but they're more powerful when you share them—and yet *even more powerful* when you share them broadly, for instance on social media. By sharing, you're instantly holding yourself accountable. But . . . perhaps you're not ready to share certain things with the people you know, like major life goals or things they'd think were out of character for you. You might fear criticism or be scared to shoulder the accountability in case you change your mind. And since we're constantly reinventing ourselves (especially in our 20s and 30s), it can be difficult for the people who've seen us through our many iterations to keep up and get on board with another version without knocking us down.

That's where this tool comes in. It guides you to share your dreams before you're ready for the accountability that comes with it. You'll show the Universe that you're serious enough to share, but protect yourself from any judgment or criticism that could kill a dream before you try.

Besides being exciting, fun, and quite stealthy, this tool is massively powerful. You're claiming to the Universe that you respect your dreams enough to share them and you're simultaneously making a statement that you believe there's enough to go around—because you'll be secretly helping someone else achieve theirs.

Directions:

- *Step 1:* **Envision**. First, envision your authentic self completely living the life you wish to live. Visualize how that makes you feel and how it makes your world different. Focus *only* on the end result, and not the steps you think it would take to get there. For the sake of this writing exercise: You're there, and it is done.

  For instance, if you want to be interviewed on the *Today* show, see yourself in Rockefeller Center talking to Matt Lauer, not writing the best-selling book that will catapult you there. The "how" is not your concern here—just the end result of your desire and how that makes you feel.

- *Step 2:* **Write**. On a piece of paper that can be ripped out of your journal (make sure nothing important is on the back), write down clearly all the details of what you envisioned above: all the dreams and goals you're afraid to admit you want because then you'd be responsible for attaining them. Share your deepest dreams for yourself; be specific and fantasize without limitations. What will you be like? Feel like? Look like? Dress like? Who will you be with? How would this impact the world around you?

- *Step 3:* **Get Set.** Rip out your piece of paper, fold it up, and write Tool No. 29 on the top.

- *Step 4:* **Field Trip!** Head to your local library or bookstore and go to the self-help section. Find another copy of *Let It Out* on the shelves. Put your folded-up journal page with your authentic dreams into that copy of the book and add in a folded dollar bill as well. Put the book back on the shelf—and flee!

  Feel all that goodness and abundance, as you've just inspired a stranger's limitless dream. Remember, abundance creates abundance.

PART V

LET IT OUT TO HEAL

Unleash Your Vibrant Health

"You are the CEO of your health."
— KRIS CARR

When we're unwell and need treatment, we often fall into the trap of thinking that a certain book, doctor, nutrition plan, coach, therapist, or technique can cure us. We're trained as a society to put all our faith into others to heal us—but in reality, only *we* can heal ourselves. If we don't have affirming beliefs and the right mind-set to begin with, even the strongest medicine and best doctors, nutritionists, coaches, and healers in the world might not be effective.

Though we've witnessed the power of the mind in healing the body again and again in numerous studies on the placebo effect, we still often forget the supremacy of our beliefs. It's simultaneously terrifying and empowering to know that we are in charge of the state of our physical and emotional body. So instead of giving our power away to others—or the opposite, pushing them away completely—we must *embrace* being in charge of the team that we choose for our own healing. Inspirational cancer thriver Kris Carr advises to have an entire team of people advocating for your wellness but affirms that at the end of the day, you are their CEO—it's *your* belief or disbelief in any modality that dictates whether, and how, it can contribute to your healing. Employing doctors, healers, and coaches for support is awesome, but you've got to believe in their work in order for it to spark change.

But let's be real for a minute. Especially in our modern day, this is more of a challenge than ever—basically every time we turn on the TV, we're bound to encounter drug commercials reminding us to be worried about countless health conditions. And when we *do* have an ailment, it's all too easy to put our attention on it because it's constantly reminding us of its presence through pain. Yet while focusing on what we don't want, we give almost no attention to what it is that we *do* want. We think way less about what healthy feels like than we think about what sick feels like. We obsess about the worst possible outcome of our illness, but what if we obsessed over the best outcome of it? What would that look like?

Whatever you're struggling with in your body—from diabetes to back pain to acne to kidney stones—your body wants to be well. You just need to unleash all that's blocking it from naturally healing itself. Again, this doesn't mean you shouldn't go to the doctor or should forgo your vitamins (in fact, quite the opposite), but it does mean that you should change your motivation from fear to *love* for your body. Rather than focusing on *What if this doesn't work?* focus on *What if it does?* Your belief in your healing modalities and health-care team is only as powerful as you think. By doing some inner work with your thoughts, and getting to the root cause of whatever you're trying to heal, you can then refocus on what you *do* desire, rather than what you don't.

In my own experience, I know that true healing begins with clearing space in your mind, and clearing away the negative. If vibrant health is your goal, merely eating well and exercising will only get you so far. In fact, you could be doing everything "perfectly" for your body, but if your thoughts are pessimistic, cruel, and judgmental toward yourself, your external state will reflect that. Our external physical health is a reflection of our internal thoughts. Every moment you spend thinking negatively or worrying about your health, you're actually visualizing the outcome you *don't* want to happen. Think what could happen if you visualized what you *do* want half as much. Whoa. Just by thinking, you can create a drastically different outcome. The mind-body connection is more powerful than we realize; I know I always tend to underestimate it.

The targeted tools in this section will guide you to visualize, with extreme clarity, exactly how you wish to be—to actually see and feel your healing occurring. They're the perfect pairing to whatever healing methods you're using, from acupuncture to Ayurveda to antibiotics. You'll envision what it would feel like to be completely healed, whatever that means to you, and these tools will enhance your confidence in whatever healing methods and healing team you've employed.

Diving into the clarity of how it will feel when your healing happens *before* it actually does is essential, because you can't get there physically until you've been there mentally. You *must* believe in your healing; your belief will direct your healing down to the daily actions you're inspired to take to support it. These tools help you get to that healing place in your mind every day, so you can soon reach it in your physical body as well.

- 30 The Feeling of Healing Freewrite
- 31 The Life Support Squad
- 32 An Honest Letter to Your Condition
- 33 The Surrender List
- 34 The Create-a-Miracle Freewrite
- 35 The F-Word Throw Down
- 36 The Emotional Purge
- 37 The Tool to Heal the World
- 38 The Self-Help Addiction Reliever
- 39 The Shame Shifter
- 40 The Awkwardness Healer

TOOL NO. 30

THE FEELING OF
HEALING FREEWRITE

In 2002, *The New England Journal of Medicine* reported a study where doctors performed surgeries on 180 patients experiencing osteoarthritis of the knee. While two groups of patients received the actual knee surgery, a third group received placebo surgery—the doctors still made an incision at the knee, but then they only went through the verbal motions of completing the procedure. Amazingly, after the surgery, the patients who were given the sham surgery improved at the same rate as the patients who got the real surgery. What's interesting about this study is not just that the placebo patients believed they received the real surgery and were "feeling the healing," but that the entire environment around them boosted their belief. For instance, the nurses who were caretaking (who didn't know who received the real surgery or not) made their patients' belief even more powerful.

Belief *is* that crucial for healing. And whether your advice comes from your doctors, your coaches, a guru, the Internet, or your mom, none of it can work until *you* believe that it can work for you. If you can't see yourself healed from the methods you're using, it means that you're doubting them in some way—and therefore sending the Universe mixed signals on whether you want healing or not. When you can visualize yourself as healed, healthy, and well, that's rad. But when you can start feeling the healing as a result of all the methods you're using—that's when the change materializes.

Directions:

- *Step 1:* Choose one physical condition that you want to heal, and write it at the top of the page. Just focus on one for now.

- *Step 2:* Make a list of all the things you're currently doing to heal the condition. Be extremely specific. For instance, if you're struggling with acne, you might write down *meditation, getting more sleep, oil cleansing my skin, eating more whole foods, not touching my face, smiling more, going for monthly facials, and using natural makeup.* Include every little detail of what you're doing that could potentially help.

- *Step 3:* Now create a separate list of anything that you *plan* on doing and hope will help. This list should include new ideas you want to try or tips you're not following consistently but believe will contribute to your healing.

- *Step 4:* Look over both your lists, and then freewrite on this question for at least 10 minutes: What would it *feel* like if all the things you're doing and plan on doing actually worked to heal you? Would you be excited? Grateful? Get in the mental space of having been healed, and really feel the emotions flow through you as you write.

- *Bonus step:* To give your belief a superboost, go to the next page and continue with Tool No. 31, "The Life Support Squad."

TOOL NO. 31

THE LIFE SUPPORT SQUAD

Whether you're a shy introvert or an exuberant extrovert, there's no denying that we all crave connection. In fact, human connection is crucial for physical and emotional healing. Think about how in tribal communities when someone in the tribe is ill, the entire community joins together to contribute to that person's healing. Or consider many native communities that come together to care for children or elders. In our Western modern society, we tend to take an opposite approach, living in isolation and keeping our health circumstances private. This is our mistake, since connection is more powerful than we give it credit for.

I mentioned the story of healing my acne and my eating disorder earlier in this book. As odd as it sounds, the most crucial piece of my healing process was sharing what I was going through with others and gaining their support. When we're honest, it's liberating. We no longer have to hide the healing quest we're on; we can instead bring others along. And having people on your side believing in your healing along with you helps *you* release any last doubt.

When I was constantly trying to hide my blemished skin, I didn't even want to be in public. I was so distracted with thoughts about it constantly. It made me question everything and was especially frustrating because while I was living this "perfect, clean, healthy, natural lifestyle" (my blog was called *The Wellness Wonderland,* for gosh sakes), my face was showing the world that something was out of whack. It made me constantly feel like a fraud, and I was always hiding my true feelings.

That's when my journal became my best friend—it was the one place I could be fully open. That honesty made me feel so good and brought me so much clarity that I realized maybe I could actually be that open with another human being. Terrified, I decided to talk to my boyfriend about what I was emotionally going through with my skin—the actual pain it was causing me and all the intense, fraudulent feelings it was bringing up in me. Outing this to someone felt like a deep exhale, and immediately I felt more at peace. And it was only after I confessed what I was going through and elicited support, that the actions I was taking to heal myself actually began to work.

You see, human connection is crucial for healing. While the condition may be yours, your healing has to be shared. In my own life, I proved this to be true time and again.

Directions:

- *Step 1:* Choose a condition that you're working to heal. It could be a physical condition, like an ailment, or an emotional one, or even a life situation that's bringing you upset. Write that in the center of a fresh page and circle it.

- *Step 2:* Make a plan for healing this condition or situation by creating a "mind map," brainstorm style. First jot down and circle everything you might need to support your healing: which people, what resources, and so forth, connecting the bubbles with lines showing how they're related. Then write down everything you're willing to do and committed to doing. Be sure to be gentle with yourself, and give simple, attainable action items rather than sweeping requests. Try to make it fun, like a quest you're about to embark on for healing and personal growth.

- *Step 3:* When you're happy with your healing mind map, ask yourself whom you can share your plan with. Identify one or more specific people to bring on board—people who will hold that healing space for you by being your support to lean on and who will check in on you during your healing quest. These people must be able to believe as much as you do in your healing or the healing of the situation. Perhaps it's a coach, your partner, a friend, a doctor, a parent, or a child— just find someone who can be there for you and hold you accountable. Either show the map to them or simply tell them about it in conversation.

- *Step 4:* Once you share your mind map, you'll now want to lock in the support you need for healing this condition or situation by creating a prayer petition to the Universe. On a separate piece of paper, and using your mind map as inspiration, write a single pointed prayer about what you would like to have occur. It could be something like this:

Dear Universe,

I know you've got a lot on your plate, but if the healing of my situation is for the highest good, please guide me in the direction I need to go for that outcome. Please send me all the support, resources, patience, and guidance needed. Thank you.

After you write this on a piece of paper, sign it.

- *Step 5:* Your mind map is completed, you've enlisted one or more people for support, and you've created a prayer petition to the Universe. What could be left? Well, there's one more thing to really cement this process: enlisting even more people in your support squad to virtually "sign" your petition.

  I got this idea from one of my favorite books, *Eat Pray Love,* where author Elizabeth Gilbert makes a petition to God for her painfully long divorce to be finalized. In her mind, she thinks of all the people who would support her petition and envisions them signing her prayer. Minutes later her phone rings; she receives the news that her divorce has been finalized and she is free. This inspired me so much that I, too, now call in support for my prayers all the time.

  So with this step, you're not going to go door-to-door with a pen; rather, look over your petition to God (aka the Universe), and think about who would hypothetically sign off on it. This can be anyone dead or alive, people you know or people you've never met but whom you think would have no problem signing your petition for your healing. Go ahead and write people's names underneath your petition prayer.

My list might include, for example, my dead grandmothers and my living grandfathers (they'd for sure want the best for me); Taylor Swift and Lena Dunham (they'd totally be all about this); my parents, aunts, uncles, and cousins (no doubt); my college roommates and all my high school friends (they'd definitely sign this for me); my teachers, principals, and coaches (they'd be proud to sign this); Oprah; Princess Grace of Monaco; Steve Jobs; my mentors; my gurus; Barack Obama, Michelle Obama, their girls, and their dogs—okay, I could go on for days enlisting support, but you get the idea. Make a list of your own support squad that feels good to you, and every time you write a name, feel their support energetically rushing in and aiding in your healing.

AN HONEST LETTER TO YOUR CONDITION

Regardless of what you're intending to heal, it is there for a reason. It's a signal from your body trying to tell you something. Just as with the alert light in your car, you can either ignore it and leave the problem to get worse, or you can look into it and start to determine *where* it came from and *why* it's showing up. Perhaps an ailment you've been having is an alert that you've been pushing yourself too hard and need to rest. Or maybe your condition is an assignment for you to learn from, in order to share your experience with and help other sufferers.

You might not have an idea of what your condition is trying to tell you, and that's okay—this is your time to let your thinking mind take a backseat, put pen to paper, and just see what comes out. Allow your subconscious to tell you what you're supposed to learn from this experience, and let it bring a new level of awareness as to why you're suffering.

Directions:

- *Step 1:* Choose a physical condition that you want to heal, and write it at the top of the page. Just focus on one for now.

- *Step 2:* Start by addressing exactly how you feel about your condition. Let it all out, including any frustrations and fears associated with it. Get specific with exactly what it feels like in your body.

- *Step 3:* Write down anything that the condition is holding you back from doing. For instance, maybe it holds you back from doing a once-favorite activity, or maybe it's preventing you from going out in public often or veering from your normal routine. This will conclude the first part of the letter, allowing you to get out any worry or negativity.

- *Step 4:* Now shift to the positives of your condition. What are some positive things associated with having this condition? For instance, perhaps someone meaningful came into your life to take care of you, or maybe you've met some friends through connecting over it.

- *Step 5:* Now, in the last paragraph, ask yourself what this condition is trying to tell you. Close your eyes, and focus on what it is trying to teach you. Put your pen to paper and just start writing or simply moving your pen; see what emerges. Let your unconscious speak.

THE SURRENDER LIST

When looking for an answer, especially when it seems urgent, we tend to push things to happen. In reality, however, the less we try, the more can happen . . . because we *allow* for more to happen. As Gabby Bernstein says, "When you try to make things happen, you block things from happening." We often try to control everything, so it's freeing to know we don't have to. We can hand some of that over to the Universe, which is pretty darn smart—and, as Marianne Williamson says, can turn an acorn into an oak tree, as well as an embryo into a baby . . . *damn that force is powerful.* When we understand that power, it's much easier to do our part: Surrender our worry and fear, and trust that what we're doing is working, and that the Universe will take care of the rest.

By surrendering to the Universe, we open up to creative possibilities and solutions that our human minds might not even fathom. Sure, take action—search for the right doctor, reach out to friends, try a new healing modality—but also be open to someone sitting next to you on an airplane, recommending an acupuncturist who healed them of the same condition. That sort of speeding up of things can happen only when you ask for help, step back, and allow.

This tool encourages you to give some control back to the Universe and surrender the ways you were trying to control the outcome. This exchange is powerful because, while you can still take action, you'll do it from a relaxed, unattached place where you trust the answer will be revealed to you . . . and that it may even come from an unexpected source. This may sound heady, but it works.

Directions:

- *Step 1:* **The Challenge.** Choose one condition or situation in your life that you'd like some healing or resolution on. It can be emotional or physical, or even a situation in your life or career. Write that at the top of your page. Then split the page into two halves by drawing a line down the middle.

- *Step 2:* **You.** On the left side of the page, list all the things that you're actively doing to try to control the situation. For instance, seeking out the ideal doctor by making phone calls and sending e-mails, asking others for help, doing several specific healing modalities, and so on. Write out every action you're taking.

- *Step 3:* **The Universe.** On the right side of the page, for each element in the left-hand column, list a way that you can let go and allow the Universe to intervene on your behalf. For instance, across from "seeking out the perfect doctor," you might write: "The Universe will bring into my life the perfect person to treat this condition in divine timing." Let yourself surrender each thing you're trying to force happen and give it up to the Universe.

THE CREATE-A-MIRACLE FREEWRITE

A pretty smart dude named Albert Einstein is reported to have said, "There are only two ways to live your life. One is as though nothing is a miracle. The other is as though everything is a miracle." True, it may seem like it'd be a miracle for your body to transform into a state of wellness, whether you're healing cancer or wanting to lose a significant amount of weight. However, a miracle may not be as dramatic as you imagine.

A Course in Miracles defines a miracle as simply a shift in perception, and says that miracles are our birthright—when they're *not* occurring, something has gone wrong. Basically, I interpret that as the lens through which we choose to look at life. By viewing life through an optimistic lens, we notice the naturally occurring synchronicities and moments of quiet bliss that are constantly around us. But when we go through life with a negative attitude, it's difficult to notice synchronicities and bliss because we're shopping for fear, worry, and despair . . . and so then that's what we see.

If you believe that your healing isn't possible, it's likely that you haven't visualized yourself doing the things you most desire or getting in touch with what that would feel like. But as author and teacher Wayne Dyer often said, when you're able to go there in the mind, you can go there in your body as well—if you believe. Your belief, and willingness to be guided, will bring you all the necessary resources and people to get you to your end result, and this tool will give you extreme clarity to tell the Universe what it is that you actually want. The *how* doesn't matter, because the *how* is not important.

Whether it's to keep up with your kids, climb Mount Everest, or build a multimillion-dollar business, be unapologetic and believe not only that you can have a physical body that supports that goal but that you are entitled to it. Remember: The Universe wants your body to be healthy and well as much as you do—in fact *it designed you to be that way,* so it will assist you in getting back to that state.

Directions:

- *Step 1:* Before you begin, close your eyes, take a deep breath, and visualize yourself doing whatever it is you most want to do. It could be physical, and you could see yourself as the healthiest version of you. Or it could have to do with your lifestyle, and you could see yourself working at your ideal career, or living in your ideal city, or in the relationship you most desire. Trust the first thing that pops into your mind, and focus solely on that.

- *Step 2:* Set a timer for 10 minutes. Let your pen flow, expanding upon this image of yourself in vivid detail and what you're doing in the world. Invite people into this image. Get specific on all the sensory qualities: what you feel like, what you're seeing and hearing, what you're wearing, what you smell like, and so on.

- *Step 3:* Immediately after completing that 10-minute freewrite, set your timer for 5 minutes and freewrite about how you'd *feel* to be completely at home in your body. Ask yourself how it would feel to have your body be fit, healthy, calm, relaxed, abundant, and well enough to do the thing that you wrote about in Step 2.

- *Step 4:* Once the five minutes are complete, close your journal. Sit in stillness for one minute to soak up the power of this tool. In your mind's eye, see yourself: vibrant, free, and healthy, with glowing skin, shining hair, your most healthy body weight, an abundance of energy, and most important, a nonjudgmental attitude about your physical self. Relax into knowing the Universe designed you to be healthy and well, so it will assist you in getting back to that state.

THE F-WORD
THROW DOWN

This is easily the toughest tool in the book—but also the most transformational. As they say in the 12-step programs, holding on to a resentment, whether toward yourself or others, is like drinking poison: It hurts only you. You are allowing it to keep you stuck.

Forgiveness can change everything.

By letting yourself be willing to forgive, you're both owning your role in keeping yourself stuck and shifting into a new way of being . . . powerful stuff. So take your time with this tool. Be patient and trust that you're on the right path when old, negative feelings that you've been hiding for years start to show up. Be gentle with yourself as you let out your resentments, and focus on one at a time; in time, they will all start to loosen and release. Don't block yourself by thinking you've forgiven all you need to or that this won't work for you. Let out your resentments, let in a new story, and most important feel better.

Directions:

- *Step 1:* **Identify your resentments.** Ask yourself: *What relationships or memories still cause me pain or sadness? What negative thoughts about myself or others does my mind repeatedly turn to? Who am I unwilling to forgive?* Freewrite on the first thing(s) that come to mind.

  Some examples of what this might look like: Your resentment could be toward others ("I blame my ex-boyfriend for hurting me, and now I think all relationships will be that way."). It could be toward a family member whom you deeply love but also resent ("I blame my parents because they never listen to me, and so I don't feel heard or good enough."). Or the resentment could be toward yourself ("I'm angry with myself because I can't get it together. I keep overeating and hating my body.").

- *Step 2:* **Dig in.** Now look over the above and freewrite on the following: *Why am I holding on to these past resentments or hurts? What would it take for me to let them go? How would it feel if I did?* Just work with one resentment at a time. If you realized you have many resentments to heal, take it slow and return to this tool again.

- *Step 3:* **Create a list of compassion.** Identify the ways in which those you resent—or yourself, if the resentment is toward you—are struggling or suffering. Put yourself in their shoes, and seek to understand why they are the way they are. When working with forgiving yourself, take a loving approach to all aspects of your life, while taking into account that your frustration toward yourself is just keeping you stuck. It's only when you can stop attacking yourself that you can then create the change you desire. This may take a bit of internal digging.

From this loving stance, create a list of compassion statements. Examples might include "I have compassion for my father because he didn't feel loved as a child and therefore didn't know how to express love to me"; or "I see why my boss is so rude to me. He is clearly under a ton of pressure from his boss and is expressing that stress to me"; or "I see why I missed that workout three days in a row. I'm on my period, and it wasn't what was best for me"; or "I see why I've been uninspired to blog lately. I'm so lonely and sad from my breakup that I just don't have the strength."

- *Step 4:* **Open to forgiveness.** You have to be willing to forgive before forgiveness can actually work its magic in your life. Simply open up to the possibility of forgiving and ask yourself, *How can I take ownership of my past hurts? How might I have brought the situation into my life or prolonged it without realizing it?* This could be anything from not speaking up when you should have or pretending that something didn't bother you when it did, to simply grasping tightly to your anger and being unwilling to let it out. Taking care of your side of the street and understanding your role in any situation is the key to moving on. Playing the role of the victim will only keep you stuck.

However, there are of course many horrific situations that occur that are completely out of your control, such as sexual assault. Your part is *only* that you allow yourself to forgive. It may seem too painful to, but to fully release the pain, open yourself to forgiveness—not for the sake of the other person, but for you.

- *Step 5:* **Create a new story.** Now that you've gone deep into a forgiveness practice, you can shift your thoughts from resentment to a new story of love and compassion. Create an affirmation to solidify your new story as it takes root. An example of a forgiving affirmation could be *I accept that my boss is under pressure, too, and I choose to let this go so that I can feel relief now.* Or, *I accept all my feelings, and I choose to let go so that I can feel relief and enjoy renewed creativity.* Or, *I understand that we all have our own paths, and I choose to let go of resentment now so I can feel relief.* Any time your thoughts start to fixate on your past resentment, your affirmation will guide your new story to take hold.

THE EMOTIONAL PURGE

You've just been hurt, wronged, and angered by a person or situation completely out of your control. You're feeling a million feelings—everything from loss to frustration to grief. What do you do? How do you cope?

This tool is your relief. It's the ultimate exercise to vigorously let it out. It guides you to let go of your pain for good by disposing of it in a bold, active, and very permanent way. By purging the emotion out of your body and mind, you can start fresh.

These two powerful steps allow you to feel your pain fully, and to release it to the trust that you have in the cosmos. By doing so, you are energetically sending a neon sign to the Universe that you are asking for not only forgiveness but also relief. This doesn't mean that you think the situation is okay, but that you're *not allowing it to hold you back anymore.* For every second you obsess about or hold on to the resentment, you're allowing it to take your power away.

The potential relief that you can feel by utilizing this tool is extraordinary, and I've seen it proven effective time and again by my clients. By completely purging the situation on paper and disconnecting from the entire episode, you can let it go and be healed. And let me tell you, it feels real good.

Note: It's important that this tool is not done on the computer. It requires the tactile, physical writing process for you to be able to authentically release everything you're holding on to here. I expect there to be all caps, crossings out, scribbles, and energy in this freewrite, and if you're typing . . . well, you could break your computer keys with all that energy.

Directions:

- *Step 1:* Grab your journal and tear out a page—yes, make sure that the page is *out* of your journal. Start to write out all the feelings that are swirling around in your mind about your emotional hurt, wrong, or wound. Allow your mind to drain, and write until you can't write anymore. (You may need to tear out additional pages after you fill up the first one—that's fine!) You'll know you're done when you feel you've said everything that there is to say about what happened and how you're feeling—not filtering a word or editing. Until that point, vigorously keep your hand moving across the page and feel the pain fully, allowing it to pour through you, one word at a time, until you've let it all out. Acknowledge with tremendous honesty all the anger, hurt, and guilt from this situation.

- *Step 2:* When you're satisfied that you've let out everything that you were holding on to, then grab a lighter or matches. Take a deep breath. Burn the freewrite from Step 1 as if you're performing a sacred, magical ritual, sending a sign to the Universe that you're releasing these negative emotions and asking for them to be removed from your mind. As you watch them go up in flames, feel the negativity evaporating from your consciousness as well. (Careful: Don't burn yourself! I've been known to set off a smoke alarm or two in my day with this one.) Acknowledge through this process not only that the wound can begin to heal, but also that there is a lesson in and reason for this wound. Even if you can't see it yet, just be open to that lesson coming to you later. I promise you, if you are open it will eventually find you.

We all have a divine open wound like this, and I truly believe that it's here to teach us something. When we stop carrying it around like a bad thing and instead let it out and burn it, we can find the lesson within the ashes. For example, when I had an eating disorder, I harbored a lot of grief and anger about my body. I desperately wished I could just be like those girls who are naturally as thin as supermodels but can eat burgers and fries and pasta and never even think about their weight. Once I finally, literally burned that anger and watched it turn to ash, I actually became grateful for the entire experience, every single bit of it. My eating disorder and relationship to my body was a massive open wound in my life that I firmly believe I came here to Earth to experience, heal, and learn from . . . and now teach others how I healed, which is part of my life's path and purpose.

THE TOOL TO HEAL THE WORLD

It's been proven that when we give to others, that feels great to us. I'm sure you've experienced this in your life countless times—I know I have. That's why this tool is really groovy. You know that giving makes you feel good, but this tool actually helps you revel in this phenomenon by tracking your emotions post-giving. It also helps you not only brainstorm random acts of kindness but also follow through with them by actually penciling them into your calendar. These random tasks could be for people you know or people you don't. Each act of kindness, however small, will compound, and every ripple of giving you send out to the world will create innumerable waves of goodness. What you put out comes back to you like a boomerang, so the more kindness you exude, the more you will receive.

This is a never-ending, self-sustaining tool where each time you complete your five tasks, you journal how you feel and then plan to do five more. It's a positive feedback loop of kindness. Just think if everyone was doing this how great the world would be. Most important, have fun with it; and if you feel inspired by it, share it on social media—you never know who you'll inspire in return. Hashtag #LetItOut #Tool37 and tag me @katiedalebout—I want to see! For every tweet I see about this tool, I'll match your kind acts by doing a kind act myself.

Directions:

- *Step 1:* List five super-simple ways in which you can make an impact in your local community and environment. Make sure that these are small enough to be doable *this month.* Examples might be loading a parking meter for a stranger, paying for the coffee for the person behind you, taking 10 minutes to pick up trash in a park on a nice day, leaving flowers on your neighbor's stoop without a note, volunteering at an urban farm, cooking dinner for a family member, or driving a friend to the airport early before the sun rises.

- *Step 2:* Grab your calendar or day planner, and write in these items for when you'll follow through with each one. Look at what and whom you'll need to help you.

- *Step 3:* Grab a sticky note or bookmark, and mark both the pages in your calendar and the page in your journal that contain the list from Step 1. Write on the note or bookmark the date that you'll complete your acts of kindness; it should be no more than one month from today's date. Flagging these pages will remind you to return to them for the follow-up steps of this tool.

- *Step 4:* As you complete each act of kindness, return to your list in your journal and write next to each task how you felt after it was completed. Notice your emotions, and just write it all down. Do this for each act you complete.

- *Step 5:* When all your tasks are complete, reflect on which one made you feel the best, the most excited, and that you've had the most fun with. Let it inspire you to write down five more acts of kindness—and be sure to share your experience on social media or with me.

THE SELF-HELP
ADDICTION RELIEVER

I once read something on Instagram that said, "I'm either completely obsessed or totally disinterested." I immediately regrammed it with the caption "Story of my life." It depicted my nature of becoming super into whatever it was that sparked inspiration in me. This has happened since I was a kid: first with the Spice Girls, listening to their songs on repeat and singing them word for word, watching their movie, *Spice World,* countless times, and being them for Halloween. Then it was with the musical *Rent,* again knowing every line, seeing it live at least seven times, and even skipping a day of school to go see the movie with my mom when it came out.

Since the Spice Girls and *Rent,* I've repeated the same pattern in my 20s with everything from yoga to raw veganism to spirituality. While this extreme passion and borderline obsessive nature has served me well in some ways (for instance, it's helped me take in an immense amount of information quickly), I also realized it could be quite limiting. That was especially the case for me with health and wellness. I was so obsessed with eating the cleanest diet, having all the superfoods, and practicing all the wellness routines I read about (from oil pulling to dry brushing to meditation) that wellness became my sole identity (like I've mentioned, my blog was called *The Wellness Wonderland,* for gosh sakes).

Health and wellness was all I talked about, read about, and honestly cared about. It was a step above even how I was with the Spice Girls (which is saying a lot because I really liked them). Alongside wellness I became deeply addicted to self-help—constantly listening to it, reading it, and even using it as entertainment—to the point where I couldn't fold laundry without taking in an inspiring podcast simultaneously. I know these things might seem innocent enough, but my laser focus was preventing me from having any other interests and being a well-rounded person. I had completely abandoned who I was before my health and personal-growth obsessions took hold, so I had no clue what else I even liked. Moreover, I wasn't even applying the information I was learning. I was simply distracting myself with it, taking in more and more to *feel like* I was changing, when really I was diverting myself from why I actually turned to self-help in the first place—the fact that I needed to deal with my emotions. As usual, I turned to my journal, and out came this tool.

It's easy to go down the rabbit hole of being "passionate" about a particular topic to where it transforms from an interest and hobby . . . to your identity. I've seen my situation mirrored in so many of my clients, too, and I designed this tool for us all. It encourages us to discover who we are, embrace our unique tastes, and own our preferences, and it guides us to find individualized pleasure outside of the narrow tube we've confined ourselves to for so long.

Directions:

- *Step 1:* Regardless of what your addiction is—it can be self-help, health, spirituality, or something else—create a pleasure list by writing down things that you enjoy doing *purely* for fun. These can be anything; however, they must be largely outside of work, fitness, and food because while that's great if you enjoy your work or workouts or meals, they're more routines that you do rather than things you've actively sought out for pure fun. Focus on things for personal enjoyment outside of both your daily routines and your hobby addictions (so if you have a self-help addiction, you can't list anything in that sphere). To get you started, here's an example of my pleasure list:

  - *Lying in the sun*
  - *Improv class*
  - *Long walks outside with friends, talking to friends on the phone*
  - *Listening to long podcasts*
  - *Listening to audiobooks on long drives*
  - *Watching YouTube videos*
  - *Attempting hair tutorials on YouTube*
  - *Scrolling through Instagram and watching Snapchat stories or Periscopes*
  - *Writing out random song lyrics in my journal*
  - *Watching reruns of* Friends

- *Going to the beach*
- *Listening to music while crying on my bed*
- *Listening to music while dancing around my apartment*
- *Going to the movies*
- *Playing the ukulele*
- *Scrolling through Pinterest*
- *Reading fiction books and personal memoirs*
- *Reading biographies*
- *Wandering around bookstores*
- *Coloring mandalas or coloring books*
- *Picnics in the park*
- *Going to farmers markets*
- *Getting tea with friends and having long conversations*
- *Recording my podcast*
- *Traveling*
- *Writing*

- *Step 2:* Whenever you need a boost of positive energy, a jolt of pleasure, or to get out of a rut, consult this list in your journal. Then *do* one or more of the things on your pleasure list. Sometimes all it takes is a gentle reminder to spark your interest and pull you out of any fixations, obsessions, or addictions to other hobbies. And the more you do your favorite things on this list, the more you'll realize how much of who you are exists outside of those addictions.

- *Step 3:* Update this list regularly, as your interests and favorite things will change as you evolve, grow, and change. These things will become your security blankets to turn to in all your intense moments. They'll make you feel less alone and more yourself because they'll get you out of your head and remind you of who you are. Since the items on your pleasure list are all so unique to you, they'll easily bring you back to your true nature when you've veered out.

THE SHAME SHIFTER

Researcher, speaker, and author Brené Brown, Ph.D., who's spent over a decade studying vulnerability, worthiness, and shame, makes a very clear distinction between shame and guilt. She defines *shame* as focus on the self, with self-talk like "I am bad," or "I am a terrible person." *Guilt,* on the other hand, focuses on the behavior, with self-talk like "That was the wrong thing to do," or "My reaction was terrible." Guilt can be productive and helpful, but shame is not; in fact, it can be very destructive.

This distinction is more than merely language. Brown teaches that shame is directly correlated to eating disorders, addiction, suicide, depression, and violence. On the other hand, guilt is inversely correlated with those. In her 2012 TED Talk, "Listening to Shame," she says about guilt, "The ability to hold something we've done or failed to do up against who we want to be is incredibly adaptive."

This tool guides you to examine your self-talk within specific scenarios, clearly observe how you speak to yourself, and shift to a more adaptive state of being. The shift from a place of shame to one of guilt is massive, and this exercise can transform your self-talk in any situation and prevent it from spiraling.

Directions:

- *Step 1:* Think of a time when you did something wrong. It can be recent or it can be something far in the past that you've been carrying or that's been haunting you. With this situation in mind, examine how you talk to yourself about it, what you say to yourself about your role in it. Write out exactly what goes on in your head.

- *Step 2:* Looking at what you've written, notice whether you're feeling shame or guilt around this situation. Remember, guilt focuses on the scenario; it is when you feel that *your behavior* was bad, and you acknowledge that you made a mistake. Shame, however, focuses on your character; it is when you feel that *you* were bad. Brown often uses the example that guilt is saying to yourself, *I _made_ a mistake,* while shame says, *I _am_ a mistake.*

    If you're feeling guilt, forgive yourself (perhaps revisit Tool No. 35), and write about what you learned from the situation. Then simply let it go. If you're feeling shame, we have some deep work to do in order to shift out of it, so please move down to Step 3.

- *Step 3:* To begin shifting your shame to a more productive place of guilt, start by becoming aware of *all* your self-talk and self-judgment around this circumstance. Awareness is key for shifting anything, so get honest about how you're speaking to yourself, and write that all down. It will probably be harsh. You'll probably want no one to see this, and you'd likely never speak to another person like you speak to yourself here. But when you can get out what you did onto paper, that takes it from swirling around in your mind and out into the light of day where you can deal with it.

For instance, perhaps in Step 1 you wrote how you felt after compulsively eating a tub of ice cream. Step 3 is the time to dig deeper and get out every bit of self-talk, as harsh as it might sound. For example, perhaps your self-talk includes: *I just can't stop myself. I'm disgusting. I have no self-control.*

- *Step 4:* Now shift that self-talk about the situation to how you would talk to a child if they did something wrong. Is there any way you would tell an innocent child the things that you tell yourself? Of course not. Even though we're grown up now, each of us was once a child and still has an inner child who needs our nurturing, empathy, and understanding.

For instance, and using the same ice cream example from above, the new self-talk might sound like: *You made a mistake. You're human; everyone overindulges sometimes and that's all right. It's no problem; you're going to get through this. It doesn't have to become a pattern. You were really stressed, and this is how you dealt with it. Next time you can make a different choice that won't give you such a tummy ache. It is going to be okay. You're okay.* In your own words, write something similar that applies to your unique situation of shame, and cross out the harsh words you were originally thinking above.

- *Step 5:* So far you've had to get incredibly honest with yourself and your journal. You've done great work. There's one more step, though, if you're comfortable keeping going. While releasing shame on paper is incredibly healing, outing yourself to someone safe is highly recommended for the deepest level of transformation.

    As Brené Brown teaches, *shame can't survive where there is empathy.* This is because shame needs you to believe you are *alone* for it to take hold in your mind. When you gain empathy from a friend, however, shame naturally releases because you know you're not alone. So speaking your shame is key. Make sure you choose a person who will be nurturing, gentle, and nonjudgmental: perhaps a family member or best friend. Share what you wrote with someone you trust . . . and watch as your shame evaporates.

THE AWKWARDNESS HEALER

In high school I would say on repeat that I was awkward. I was a self-identified awkward person around boys, teachers, and people in general. This phrase became my crutch. What I didn't realize then (but know now) was that my awkwardness was only true because *I made it true.* Feeling awkward only happens when we're not being ourselves.

My best friends from high school, Ellen and Maria, taught me something valuable. They'd say, "It's only awkward if you make it awkward." I don't know if they made this up or read it in a fortune cookie, but either way it became our new outlook going forward; the three of us simply decided not to define anything as awkward anymore. Of course we had uncomfortable situations arise, but the three of us chose to laugh at them rather than cringe with awkwardness.

To be honest, the only reason I felt so damn awkward when I was younger was because I was trying too hard—to be cool, liked, and accepted—when in reality, the times I was most accepted and liked were when I was most vulnerable and real.

A foolproof plan to avoid any feelings of awkwardness is to simply be real. If you're silly, be silly. If you're serious, be serious. But whatever you do, don't try to be something that you're not—*that's* when things get awkward. If you're feeling confident and being authentic, you'll naturally inspire the people around you to be themselves, too. Just like everything else in life, you have a choice in any moment. So even if you find yourself in a weird one, you can choose to laugh, be present, be yourself, and let the moment be what it is. Maybe you even say how you're feeling. Outing your feelings helps them dissipate, as I mentioned in Tool No. 39. My favorite podcast is called *You Made It Weird* with Pete Holmes; the entire premise of the show is based on awkward moments. Why? Because *that's* where we show our humanity most; *that's* what we can connect on most, making us all feel a little less alone.

Directions:

- *Step 1:* Think back to an awkward conversation or situation you found yourself in. It can be recent or from years ago. Write down the story of what happened and what the awkwardness or embarrassment felt like.

- *Step 2:* Similar to shame, as we went over in Tool No. 39, I believe awkward feelings can't survive when you share them—because when you share an awkward moment with someone, it simply becomes a silly one. Laughing at yourself is the best medicine, so share your awkward story with a friend. Or, like in Tool No. 29 ("The Coolest Tool in the Book"), tear out the page, fold it up, and leave it on this page in a copy of this book in a bookstore or library for a lucky reader to find and get a big laugh out of. Most important, be sure to allow *yourself* to fully laugh and feel the silliness of the situation as you share your story.

Note: This tool is best utilized on the spot. So, the next time you find yourself in an awkward situation or encounter (and you know you will), remember this exercise and the experience of sharing your awkwardness, and consider sharing your feelings live, right there in the moment. Chances are that if you feel awkward, other people in the situation probably do, too . . . and maybe you can all just transform the tension into silliness right then and there.

PART VI

LET IT OUT TO FEEL

Beyond Fear to New Highs

"Life is supposed to be a series of peaks and valleys. The secret is to keep the valleys from becoming Grand Canyons."
— BERNARD WILLIAMS

Uncertainty is a reality of life. Anything we haven't done before really flips out our species, and rightfully so. It's difficult to wrap your mind around something you have no concept of. Think of babies, the first time they get the hiccups. They flip out because they're completely uncertain of what's going on within them. But now when you get the hiccups, you don't sweat it (I hope) since you've gotten them countless times before and know with certainty they'll eventually pass.

But unlike with the hiccups, we don't have that same certainty that everything will work out in other uncomfortable situations in our lives.

Most fear is actually uncertainty in disguise, and to conquer our fears and reach new levels of success, we must move outside our comfort zone—right into the spot where uncertainty and fear set up camp. There's no kicking them out; you just have to get cozy with them, and the tools in this section will guide you in doing so.

You might even eventually trade in fear and uncertainty for pure excitement. I've heard many times before that fear and excitement feel the same in our bodies—we just interpret the two emotions in very different ways.

Let me give you a warning up front: This section is not for dabblers. Prepare yourself for powerful, fear-quashing, confidence-building techniques that I myself continue to use and that have catapulted me to new highs way outside my comfort zone. They've proven effective for releasing fear when practiced consistently. I use these techniques daily and turn to them—rather than food, work, shopping, [insert your default coping method of choice here]—when I'm in a funk of fear, worry, and anxiety. Remembering to use them takes work, like building a muscle, and has finally become intuitive for me, but it took patience. Once you start to use journaling as a solution and see the dramatic results, these tools will become your default response to fear as well.

I want to be clear: I'm not perfect—I don't journal always at the first sign of discomfort. I still have bad days where I turn to old coping mechanisms rather than solving by journaling. I don't beat myself up about it, though, because that would take me farther down that negative path, requiring *even more* journaling to recover. Instead, I gently return to my journaling practice without adding the guilt from forgetting. I grab my journal, usually using the tools in this section, and start solving the puzzle of fear in my mind. I share this because I don't want you to beat yourself up for not wanting to use these tools in the moment or choosing instead to cope rather than solve. That's okay. These will be here for you when you're ready for them. If you beat yourself up for beating yourself up, you're wasting your time and keeping yourself stuck. So just come back to these tools when you're ready, and know it was in divine perfect timing. Everything is.

This section isn't all about fear; it's about its opposite, love, as well. Many of the tools guide you to release fear simply by opening up to love. Sometimes what we fear most is simply claiming what we want, stating our desires, and being brave enough to go after them. Author and teacher Marianne Williamson says, "Our deepest fear is not that we are inadequate. Our deepest fear is that we are powerful beyond measure. It is our light, not our darkness, that most frightens us. We ask ourselves, Who am I to be brilliant, gorgeous, talented, fabulous? Actually, who are you *not* to be?"

These tools lead you to claim what you love, beat uncertainty, and step into the wholeness of who you really are and who you're meant to be. Basically, they're going to help you fully shine. They're the polish to the beautiful silver that is you, stripping away dullness from wear over time and returning you to the sparkling self you are underneath that.

So before pulling out the big guns and forging ahead into this section of the book, ask yourself these preliminary questions: *Am I willing to tackle uncertainty head-on to take my life to new highs? Am I done with fear?* As spiritual teacher Sonia Choquette says, it's not fear that keeps us stuck; it's hiding fear. So with that, are you ready to stop hiding fear and let me help you let it out?

Then let's go.

- 41 The Stepping-on-Fear Steps
- 42 The Love List
- 43 The Perfect Match
- 44 The Pre-Breakup Gut Check
- 45 The Affirmation Write-Out
- 46 The Fear-Quashing Worksheet
- 47 The Mourning Tool
- 48 The Emo Tool

THE STEPPING-ON-FEAR STEPS

If you wait for everything to be perfect, you'll be waiting forever. Perfectionism can just be a disguise for procrastination. When I wanted to start a podcast, I had no clue how to do it or really even what one was, but in the words of Yogi Bhajan, "When the time is on you, start, and the pressure will be off." So I just started, doing one thing at a time, asking for help along the way, figuring it out as I went, and pushing myself to keep going even when I had no clue where it would go. Fast-forward to now: I've grown my podcast substantially, hosted some awesome people, and today it's one of my favorite things I do.

Getting started gives you momentum, and this tool makes what may seem like a big process manageable by breaking it down into small, actionable steps. The only way to move through fear is by taking one small step in the right direction at a time. New pieces of information will present themselves only *after* you begin, so in that way, taking inspired action through your fear is like solving a mystery: You get only one clue (or actionable item) at a time.

All that you need will reach you, but you have to get clear on what you want and start on your path of getting there. Lean into your fear and use it as a road sign to tell you exactly where to go. Ready? Get set. Start.

Directions:

- *Step 1:* Write down a specific fear you have that holds you back from doing something you really desire. Let me illustrate this process with an example: Say you want to start a business online, but your fear is quitting your full-time job because you're afraid of not having a steady income.

- *Step 2:* Write down a single, actionable item that moves you in the direction of your fear. Be sure not to make this action too big. It should be a small step. Make it something you can handle and even do right now. For example, the action item that moves you in the direction of your fear could be as simple as deciding on the name of your business.

- *Step 3:* Follow through on this action item immediately. Close this book and move on to Step 4 only after you've completed it.

- *Step 4:* Congratulations! You've taken a step in the direction of your fear. Reflect in your journal how it feels to start and on your state of momentum after having completed your first action item. Then, cross off the action item from Step 2, and write down the *next* step you could take in the direction of your fear. Again, write just one step;

this is *not* a list you're making. The completion of each step will naturally lead you to the next. Using our example above, the next action you take, for instance, could simply be buying your website name.

Repeat Steps 2–4 to move further and further through your fear. You'll notice that with each small step you take, the more it will dissolve.

TOOL NO. 42

THE LOVE LIST

Note: This tool is a prerequisite to Tool No. 43.

I believe love is the opposite of fear. This is the main concept of the metaphysical text I study, *A Course in Miracles.* By focusing on creating more love, you naturally start to eliminate fear through "subtraction by addition." Pretty cool, right?

Manifesting and experiencing love in all your relationships is only possible when you fully and deeply love and accept yourself above all. That's why this self-love tool is a prerequisite for all the techniques for calling in loving relationships. Until you love yourself, you cannot accept the love of another. You might attract your ideal mate, but you won't feel their love if you don't believe that you deserve it. You also might attract a partner who likewise doesn't love him- or herself, since we attract in our likeness. Focusing on creating a loving relationship with *yourself* first and foremost is key to manifesting all sorts of positive relationships.

Now, in honesty, I thought this "self-love thing" was a big cheesy sham when I first heard about it, and just thought I'd avoid that piece of personal-growth work. Then I realized, self-love *was* the root of all the great spiritual and personal-growth work I was consuming. It was the missing piece for everything else I was reading and listening to, trying to take shape in my life.

Self-love isn't something to "master"; rather, it's a journey. And once you've started on your self-love journey, you can invite in a romantic relationship that can guide you to deepen that relationship of love with yourself (enter Tool No. 43).

Directions:

- *Step 1:* Create a list of things that you adore about yourself. They can be physical or emotional. They can be qualities and attributes, personality traits, and accomplishments. Your list can be as long as you like; just let your pen flow, even if it feels awkward at first (it's great to keep this list handy on your smartphone). Ideally, it should be long. Every time you return to this exercise, it should grow.

- *Step 2:* Fold this list up, and carry it with you to look at whenever you feel judged, or whenever you judge yourself. Add to this list often, as what you love about yourself will expand the more you focus on creating a loving relationship with *you.* Make sure the list is current and authentic.

- *Step 3:* After working on your love list for at least a week, ask yourself the following question: Where are you still *not* loving yourself? Freewrite your answer for at least 10 minutes.

- *Step 4:* Based on what you wrote in Step 3, notice the areas of your life that could use a little more love. Reflect on how you can view these areas as simply inspiration to work toward but still approve of yourself *regardless*. This will retrain your mind to default to self-love even when you're not perfect (which we never really are).

For instance, if you realize you still don't love that you're disorganized, you might write something like: "Even though I hate how disorganized I am, I'm choosing to approve of myself anyway. It's okay to not be perfect, and I'm moving toward organization by having this awareness, and for that I'm proud." Do this for each area of your life where you feel you could use a little more self-love.

THE PERFECT MATCH

Note: Tool No. 42 is a prerequisite for this tool.

Spiritual teacher and author Gabrielle Bernstein often says that relationships are our greatest assignments for personal and spiritual growth. They challenge us to rise to the occasion of being our best self. At the same time, for many of us they're also major points of fear (also known as excitement).

When you're loving your life—every minute of it—you become a powerful attracter of everything you desire. You're basically a shiny magnet, and your ideal romantic partner is iron shavings. However, if your magnet is dirty or blocked, the metal won't move toward it; you will have difficulty attracting the partner you desire . . . or end up with a partner who is not a good match at all. To attract your perfect match, you have to become the kind of person you want to be with; *you must become a perfect match to what you desire.*

This tool helps you find your ideal partner by first helping you get hyper-clear on what you desire and then figuring out if you're aligned with it. If not, you'll get in gear to become the type of person you'd want to be with to allow them to flow right in—just like the metal to the magnet.

Sound complicated? Don't worry. I'll guide you through all of this. You've got this.

Directions:

- *Step 1:* Create a list of things that you want in a partner. This should be fun, so have a ball! Get specific on how your partner might look, dress, act, smell. Where do they live? What do they do? What do they think of you? Don't hold back.

- *Step 2:* Look over your list, and then freewrite on the most important question of all: How do they make you *feel?* How do you feel around them? What are you like as a result of being part of this relationship?

- *Step 3:* File this list and feel free to add to it during the week. Envision it in meditation, throughout the day at work, or even while dining or exercising, and enjoy it. However, hold it just loosely in your mind. If you cling too tightly to one single vision, you might block something even greater from coming in. (Remember: We dream only a fraction of what the Universe has in store for us.)

- *Step 4:* After a week or two of holding space for this vision, create a new list of what *your life* would be like with this partner in it. How would it be different from the life you're living now? How would it be the same? How would *you* be different? How would you be the same? Would you shave your legs more? Would you dress up more around the house?

- *Step 5:* Now look over your list from Step 4 and notice if there are any gaps between how you envision your life would be with this person in it versus how your life is now. The trick to calling in the love that you crave from Steps 1 and 2 is for your answers to Step 4 to be aligned with the life you live now. If you *do* identify a large gap between how your life is now and how you envision it to be with this partner in it, move on to Step 6.

- *Step 6:* Freewrite on how you can close the gap. How can you bring more of that person-you-would-be-with-a-partner into your life *now*? How would you carry yourself if you had your ideal partner by your side? How would you act, think, dress, speak, and so on? Reflect on ways you can embody this person right now and going forward.

Remember, your ideal partner can magnetize to you only when you feel *now* how you will feel once they arrive. Having the partner you desire and wrote about should be the cherry on top of your delicious ice cream—not the ice cream itself. In other words, regardless of whether you have this person, your life should be designed in such a way that you're in a constant state of joy and love. That's when the real magnetizing takes place.

THE PRE-BREAKUP GUT CHECK

Relationships are tricky. They are complicated. They are wonderful and terrible. They grow, they change, they bend, and sometimes—yes, they break.

Breakups suck. They are seriously the worst. Anyone who says otherwise is lying. And knowing whether or not to end a relationship is a decision that brings up a ton of fear, doubt, and emotion. It's possible to have a relationship that looks perfect on paper and even seems perfect on the outside, but you're just not feeling it anymore . . . and you're not sure what to do since nothing is inherently wrong. Being honest with yourself about what you're feeling, and not simply settling for a relationship that's "not bad" but not necessarily awesome, takes courage—and will not come without emotion.

We often don't want to feel these negative, sad emotions pre-breakup, so we soothe ourselves with a couple of other guys (commonly Ben, his bud Jerry, and a spoon). While some of us eat over these feelings, some of us drink over them, some of us get into a replacement relationship over them, and some of us do a little bit of it all. Eventually though, you have to feel it, or the emotion will remain stuck inside of you. Also, it's likely that if something feels off to you in your relationship, the other person feels that in some way, too; so allowing it to bubble up to the surface is actually best for everyone.

When you have that itch that something isn't going quite right anymore and you're not sure whether to end a relationship, this tool is the gut check to confront those tough questions you're procrastinating answering for yourself. Honestly answering these questions will give you the clarity you seek and help you make sense of all the emotions associated with the breakup process as well. This tool will guide you to know whether your relationship needs to end or simply take a new form, like a relationship version 2.0. Either way a change needs to happen, because staying stagnant will only hold you both back.

Directions:

- *Step 1:* The ideal time to do this is right before bed. Give yourself some quiet time and space away from your partner to ponder your feelings and get some perspective. Perhaps take an evening walk or a bath first, and then cozy up with your journal.

- *Step 2:* Answer the following tough questions. They are deep, so it's crucial you take your time and answer them honestly and from your own intuition. Don't worry here about the consequences of taking action. Purely get clarity on how you're feeling.

  - *Is there still physical attraction in this relationship?*

  - *What are you most afraid of in leaving this relationship?*

- *What is holding you back from ending or making a change in this relationship?*

- *What would this relationship need to heal? What would it need to change?*

- *Is there more for you to learn in this relationship?*

- *Do you want to make change together or apart?*

- *What does this relationship give you? What is it abundant in?*

- *What does this relationship <u>not</u> give you? What is it lacking?*

- *Can you get what you're lacking within this relationship, or is that not possible? Why?*

- *What are you not giving to the relationship? How are you holding back?*

- *What is your partner not giving? How are they holding back?*

- *What's your favorite part of the relationship?*

- *What's your least favorite part of the relationship?*

- *Step 3:* After you've completed all the questions above, close your journal and set it aside. Sleep on it before making any decisions or having any tough conversations. Surrender and ask the Universe to guide you through whatever tough choice you must make, and know that if you are listening to your intuition fully, you can never be wrong.

THE AFFIRMATION WRITE-OUT

This tool is a writing meditation, so I encourage you to sit down, light a candle, brew a cup of tea, or even take your journal out into nature, and enjoy it. The power of this tool is in its repetitiveness; with every line you write, you are reprogramming your subconscious mind. And the more you focus, the more it can help you shift a pattern you want to change quickly.

I designed this tool intuitively. As a child I would write out my spelling words over and over again down the page to learn them so I could get them correct on the spelling test. This is much like that, but with really high-vibe statements, or affirmations. The more you write them out, the more they become part of you.

We all learn in different ways, but for me, writing things down helps me remember them more clearly and deeply. I was always the type of student who took copious notes, almost unnecessarily so, just because it helped me retain the information better. If you relate to that, this is the tool for you. (And if not, try it anyway. It might surprise you.)

Directions:

- *Step 1:* Grab a cup of tea and the journal you'll be using (I like to have a designated "affirmations journal" for this exercise specifically, but any journal will do).

  Important: This tool works best in a physical journal and requires hand-to-page effort for optimal effectiveness. The act of writing is much more active than typing on a keyboard or your phone; it will allow you to put more emotion, power, and intention behind your words. Think: teachers forcing students to repeatedly write sentences on the chalkboard until they remember them—same concept.

- *Step 2:* Decide on something you're working on in your life—something you want to change, grow, transform, or expand—and create an affirmation. It can be as specific or general as you want, but there are a few guidelines to crafting affirmations that are effective:

  1. Write the affirmation in **present tense**, as if it is already happening. For example, *I build my business with ease*, rather than *I will have a business someday.*

  2. Make sure it is something you actually want **right now**. For instance, if you want to have a baby someday but not for a while, don't make your affirmation *I am a mother.* Affirmations should be things you would be ready to invite into your life immediately.

3. Make the affirmation **believable**. If you want to feel great about your body but have a ways to go, instead of writing *I have the perfect body*, write: *I am moving toward perfect health daily.*

Step 3: Once you've crafted the affirmation that feels best to you, write it at the top of a fresh page.

Step 4: Begin copying that affirmation down the page, saying the words in your mind as you write and fill the entire page with them.

Step 5: Notice how you feel as you repeat the affirmation on the page, and allow it to change and expand as you write it more and more and believe it more and more. Allow it to evolve as you go. Stay in the flow and be relaxed.

For instance, the transition could look something like this:

I build my business with ease.

I build my business with ease.

I build my business with ease.

I build my business easily and effortlessly.

All the time, space, people, and resources flow to me.

I am abundant.

My opportunities flood me.

My business serves the world.

I create my business with flow and ease, and it serves a mass audience.

I love my work and my work loves me.

I was born to have my own business.

I am fully supported in my own business.

I think like a business owner.

I build my business easily and effortlessly.

The more you do this on paper, the more you'll be able to entrain your mind . . . and the sooner your physical, external circumstances will follow suit.

THE FEAR-QUASHING WORKSHEET

(The Most Powerful Tool in the Book)

Affirmations are amazing (as you see on the previous page, I have an entire tool and journal devoted to them), but when you're dealing with deep fears, they miss a step. You can't simply toss an affirmation over a fear—it's like putting a "Band-Aid on a bullet hole."

When working through a fear, I pull out the big guns with this fear-quashing exercise, because fears need to be *deeply examined* in order to be released. Without holding them up, figuring out where they came from, and feeling the frustration, your fears will stay stuck. Only by examining them can you change them.

This is a difficult thing to do without guidance. The fears that plague us are the things we don't want to look at or feel, so instead we eat over them, do drugs over them, watch TV over them, or whatever it is for you—anything not to have to look them in the face and feel them.

This tool puts that mirror right up to your face and guides you step-by-step to get clear about your fear, understand that it's false, and finally release it. It's a system I use constantly, because fears are always present, and always will be—they are a part of life. While it's an intense practice, the more you do it, the more you'll be able to quash fear every time it comes up. Quashing fears allows you to change them into empowering mirrors to learn from, rather than leaving them as tricky parasites that hold you back. You'll be able to appreciate your fears as signals that there's something you need to focus on, release, and heal so that you can gain a fresh perspective and ultimately move into your purpose more deeply.

Directions:

- *Step 1:* Complete this sentence:

  The fear that is stuck in my mind is _____
  _____.

  I'll walk you through with an example. Say for this you determine: *The fear that is stuck in my mind is* <u>that the only way to earn money is</u> <u>by working hard for a company at least 40 hours</u> <u>per week. I'll be stuck doing this the rest of my life.</u> <u>Entrepreneurship isn't an option for me.</u>

- *Step 2:* Define where this fear came from. Keep in mind that you'll probably have to go back into childhood, as that's when most beliefs are formed—in fact, most of our core beliefs about ourselves are fully formed prior to age eight.

  For example, perhaps you remember that when you were little, your parents were never around because they were working all the time just to make ends meet. They constantly told you and your siblings, "You have to work hard for your money."

- *Step 3:* When you think of this fear, where do you feel it in your body, physically? Make note of that.

- *Step 4:* Freewrite on how often you think about this fear. When does it come up? Where are you? What triggers it?

- *Step 5:* Now take the specific fear, and complete this sentence:

This fear is completely fake and does not actually exist, because _____.

For instance, using our example above, after reflecting on this fear you might realize: *This fear is completely fake and does not actually exist, because <u>many people DO make money by working far fewer hours. That just wasn't modeled to me as a kid, but it was certainly modeled in many other families. I've only believed working less or becoming an entrepreneur was impossible for me because I had no models otherwise</u>.*

Get super specific and break down why this fear is made up and false.

- *Step 6:* Now feel the fear intensely. Imagine a scenario where it comes up, and dive into the emotions that arise in you. By letting the fear surface completely while you're in a safe place, you allow the fear to start to loosen . . . and release. Sit in meditation, go out for a walk, head to a yoga class, or simply listen to a song with the intention of feeling all your frustration for having that fear in the first place. Let it out completely.

- *Step 7:* Now, put pen to paper again. This time, freewrite about how it feels to have examined the fear and really felt it. Is it fully released? If so, what does letting go of the limiting fear that was holding you back allow you to do? How does releasing this old belief open up new possibilities for you? What are you excited to take action on now after letting this go?

Note: Even if your fear doesn't yet feel completely released, how can you take action as if it was? As Kurt Vonnegut says, "We are what we pretend to be, so we must be careful about what we pretend to be." Sometimes you have to fake it that you don't believe in your fear anymore . . . until eventually you're not faking it—you *actually* don't believe in it.

THE MOURNING TOOL

The world is a significantly different place than it was even 5 years ago, and your life probably looks entirely different than it did 5, 10, and 20 years ago. We're meant to go through change and transitions in our lives, in our emotions, and, very visibly, in our bodies. That's the beauty of life. Think about it: You were the size of a loaf of bread, and now you're a full-grown human, but through it all it's been *you* all along.

The beautiful thing about change is that everyone around you is changing and aging, too. There's a movie called *The Age of Adaline* in which the protagonist, played by Blake Lively, doesn't age. While this may seem like an amazing gift, the story actually chronicles how difficult her life is and how she's unable to connect deeply with people as they change yet she remains stagnant.

So you see, change is inevitable, but it's also wonderful . . . and challenging. I have this cool app called Timehop on my phone that allows you to see on any given day what you posted on social media on that day each past year. At first I thought it would be a fun way to see what I was doing a year back on Instagram, but it ended up having a profound impact on me and really got into my head, especially with triggering my eating disorder. I would open it up only to judge my current body against the one in the app, comparing my current self to my past self. I quickly realized something as a result of this tool: Although I didn't want to go back to that point in time, I did need to mourn the loss of that body and who I was then.

As simple as that sounds, it took conscious effort. Looking at the photos of myself, I remembered not just what I looked like but also the extreme restriction, obsession with food, and total isolation that went into achieving it. I knew I had to embrace where I was now, mourn the loss of what was, and stop comparing my present self to my past self in order to move on. Nostalgia is natural and so is change, and how we deal with change directly dictates our happiness.

For you, it might not be body image; it might be missing the freedom of childhood, or the novelty of a relationship, or the way the world was when you were younger. Regardless of what it is that you're nostalgic for, it's time to mourn it so you can release it, which is the only way to full presence . . . which is the only way to true happiness, at least that I can figure out. This tool helps you see the beauty in change and embrace it, offering a powerful emotional release where you notice the present and welcome the new, rather than dwell stuck in the past.

Directions:

- *Step 1:* Write down all the things you miss: things about the world you live in today, or specific things about your particular life circumstances. Let yourself get nostalgic. Allow one thing you miss to turn into another; watch them multiply.

    For instance:

I miss bookstores. I miss the big Barnes & Noble that was right downtown, and how I'd walk in there and spend hours looking through magazines. I miss having time to do things like that. I miss college. I miss my college roommates and our house. I miss the way my body used to look then and my clothes fitting me so well. I miss being able to do whatever I wanted, especially spending all day by the pool without having anywhere to be. I miss not having e-mail or social media on my phone. I miss not being so aware of my emotions and just being as present as a child.

- *Step 2:* Look over what you wrote, and write down all the emotions you feel. Perhaps sadness, frustration, loss, and loneliness come up. Just write whatever washes over you.

- *Step 3:* Now replace those negative, wistful emotions with positive feelings about all that you have now. Notice the contrast.

  For instance:

I miss bookstores, *but I love that I can listen to audiobooks so easily on my phone now, and always have them with me. I can listen to them for hours on long walks.*

I miss my college times, *but I'm happy that I still have all of those friends, and that social media allows me to feel close to them.*

I miss the way my body used to look when I was younger and my clothes fitting me so well, *but my body now is healthy and strong and does so much for me. I know how to dress it well and love how I feel as much as how I look now, which is powerful since my body will constantly, continually change.*

I miss being able to do whatever I wanted in the summers and spend all day by the pool without having anywhere to be, *but being an adult is actually really freeing and supporting myself is liberating—I love having no curfew or bedtime or anyone to answer to.*

I miss not having e-mail or social media on my phone, *but it's really convenient to be able to work from anywhere in the world, and what would I do without GPS if I got lost? It's amazing.*

I miss not being so aware of my emotions and just being as present as a child, *but it's actually cool to be so awake and self-aware so I can feel the full spectrum of emotions.*

THE EMO TOOL

Emotions that don't get let out of us end up setting up camp not only in our minds but also in our physical bodies. For instance, we might hold stress in our low back, causing pain; or worry in our stomach, causing digestive problems; or fear in our hips. There are many physical pain symptoms related to emotional trauma. (Two great resources about this are *The Tapping Solution* and *You Can Heal Your Life.*) When I'm teaching my yoga classes the pigeon pose, which opens the hips, I often warn my students that long-buried emotions may come up. We hang on to lots of old emotions in our hips (other places, too, but hips are a common place emotions get stuck and why so many of us experience tight hips), and if they don't get released by being *felt,* they can create tension in our bodies.

This tool will help you relieve that. It allows you to break down your emotions, one by one, so that they're not so overwhelming and you can let them out of you completely. You'll feel a sense of release and relief after using this tool, as it will create an opening for you where the emotion can begin to drain out, no longer pent up and accumulating.

Directions:

- *Step 1:* Define the emotion you've been feeling the most lately. It's important to just choose one, even if you've been feeling a lot of different things. It could be either positive or negative. It could be anything from bliss, to jealousy, to anger, to loneliness.

- *Step 2:* Complete the following sentences using the emotion you chose to focus on in Step 1:

    - *I am feeling ___[write your emotion here]___ .*

    - *My _____ feels like . . .*

    - *My _____ acts out by . . .*

    - *My _____ came from . . .*

    Here's an example using the emotion loneliness:

    - *I am feeling lonely.*

    - *My loneliness feels like . . .*

. . . a quiet sadness from not having anyone to talk to and feeling unsupported. I feel alone even when I'm around people. I feel it in my stomach and chest like there's something built up, and I just want to turn to someone and cry to release whatever's in there. It feels like nostalgia, constantly missing people and situations where I felt supported and embraced. It feels like fear and worry about the future and how long this feeling will last.

- *My <u>loneliness</u> acts out by . . .*

. . . me feeling disorganized in all I want to do, but also feeling sad and sorry for myself since I have no one to share with, relax with, or celebrate with. This emotion acts out by forcing me to feel stuck by not fully stepping into my full potential because I don't have anyone cheering me on or pushing me further. It acts out by me turning to food for comfort, pleasure, and release when what I'm really craving is connection, support, and security.

- *My <u>loneliness</u> came from . . .*

. . . purposely isolating myself. I have a fear, which I picked up during childhood, of getting too close to people. Being left out in middle school and kids stealing my ideas is an event that turned into a belief that I shouldn't share, and that I should do everything myself. I picked up this idea like Velcro, and now it keeps me at a distance from people because I realize I'd rather be lonely than get hurt.

- Step 3: Now reflect on how it feels to have broken down that emotion. Perhaps visualize the emotion physically releasing from your body. What I like to do is watch in my mind's eye the pain from that emotion slowly dissipate. I see it like dirt in the wind spiraling out from my chest (or wherever you feel your emotion or pain) into the air. As it leaves I feel relief. And it feels rad.

PART VII

LET IT OUT TO REVEAL

Radical and Raw Solo-Therapy

"You will never be able to escape from your heart.
So it's better to listen to what it has to say."
— PAULO COELHO

I said at the beginning of this book that journaling saved me. That may sound dramatic, but it's true. Journaling is the reason that I'm functioning today, and the tools in this last section are the most powerful ones in this book, and have been the most life-changing for me.

I want to get real with you guys and share something deeper about my story from earlier that I think is relevant to see how heavy and pervasive some issues were for me, and how real and raw I allowed myself to get on the page. I also share this to show how deeply authentic you must get with *yourself* for the tools in this section to reveal to you what you need to know.

As I recounted in the Introduction, since I was a child, my biggest demon has been body hate and internalized fat phobia. At the height of my body-hate spiral and eating disorder, I was so afraid of gaining weight—weight I knew I desperately needed.

Eventually I returned to my pre–disordered eating weight and then went beyond it . . . and I wished my life would just end if I had to live at this higher weight. I had no worth outside of my body, so if I had to live in this new bigger body, I didn't want to live at all. I didn't want to be seen; I hid from cameras and spent most of my time alone in my apartment, hiding behind my computer. I'd isolated myself during my anorexia because no one wanted to hang out with a girl more into food and her body than them. I had identified as an ultra-thin person for so long, and in that body I was able to feel confident and even love myself for the first time in my life—but it wasn't real love.

The self-love I felt there was conditional. The only reason I felt okay with myself was because during that time my body fit into society's "standard of beauty," and when it didn't anymore, I believed I was back in my extreme self-hate. In my warped-by-society mind, fat was "bad," and thin was "good." I equated fat with loneliness and fear, while thin meant loved, revered, and beautiful. There wasn't just one thing that made me come to these conclusions; rather, these messages are fed to us on the regular by the media. Even in Disney movies like

The Little Mermaid, Ursula, the only fat character, is portrayed as evil. I saw people rush to my aid when I was at my eating disorder weight; but as I gained the weight back, I was completely alone, cementing my worst fears about what I had made fat mean.

I was stuck. I had to choose between going back into my anorexia or learning to be okay with myself in my new bigger body. Why couldn't I feel good about myself at my natural weight? What was I so afraid of?

In this extreme time of questioning everything, I decided to turn to my journal for a very deep conversation with myself, probing my mind with questions and responding with raw and honest answers . . . which were sometimes dark, but always very real.

To unearth my most core beliefs that were causing me all this pain, I wrote down the things I thought on repeat—things that, until now, I didn't want to admit, even to myself. You guys, *beliefs stem from repeated thoughts*; eventually, these thoughts become ingrained in our subconscious mind and run on autopilot, regardless of whether they're true or not. Many beliefs develop during childhood and are with us for so long that it takes deep journaling work to clear them.

The thoughts that had plagued me from childhood led to core beliefs that I had about myself and my self-worth:

- I'm bigger than my friends (therefore I'm not good enough).

- Boys don't like me because I'm bigger than other girls (therefore I'm unlovable).

- My hair and nose look different from everyone else (therefore I don't fit in).

- I have no value because I'm not smart or thin and that's what's valued (therefore I don't deserve attention).

Basically, I had one major core belief—*I'm not good enough as I am.* My writing revealed to me that I thought all love was conditional, and therefore I was unlovable if I was truly myself. I believed, *They will love me and listen to me only if I lose enough weight, and only if I get famous enough will I feel worthy to be loved.*

Through my writing, I also discovered a huge realization that changed everything for me:

I was more afraid of getting fat than I was of dying.

Once I saw that line on the page and the thought out of my head, something clicked, and my life changed. I was so disgusted that I ever thought this. While I could love people of any weight in my life, I had an internalized fat bias toward myself. I had been hiding it completely, not just from everyone around me but from myself. I hadn't been able to admit it because in my mind I wasn't allowed to feel that way; it seemed so awful and cruel that I held it in for years. While intellectually I knew that weight doesn't determine worthiness or lovability, this belief existed much deeper than that— and journaling was able to pull it out into the light. I realized through journaling that the reason I was so afraid of being judged is that deep down I had been judging others and was therefore judgmental toward myself.

While I was terrified of anyone ever finding out that deepest, darkest secret of mine (and now it's in a book for all to read, which still terrifies me, but I share it because I think it can be helpful to see my process and relief), by simply letting it out, it could finally dissipate. From there I was able to understand that I had a deep body-image sickness that wasn't worth dying over, and that I needed professional help. This catalyzed me to seek out the help I needed, which might not have happened had I not first discovered and observed my thoughts on the page and realized the beliefs that were running my mind subconsciously. Letting them out of my head and onto the page gave me the immediate awareness, which led to the relief I needed to begin to release them from consuming my every move.

One of my favorite authors, Nancy Levin, said something on my podcast that hit home: "Admit to yourself what you already know to be true." Self-honesty is key to happiness, and that's what I did in my journal when I got super raw and real.

This became a frequent practice of mine. I would take significant issues and work them out in my journal. The questions I asked myself became my tools I'd turn to, which eventually became the tools for this book. These prompts were and continue to be my savior, my sanity, my tools . . . and, now, your tools. I believe they came through me to not only save my life, but to benefit and perhaps even save yours in some way, too.

I share this unfiltered aspect of my story in hopes of showing how radically deep, real, and honest you must get with yourself in order for these tools to reveal to you what you need to know, learn, and even maybe, when you're ready, teach.

What I've found with my clients and the work I've done on myself is that there's usually one specific fearful issue that's consistently revealed to you through each exercise almost every time your pen hits your journal. The more you practice journaling, the more you will start to observe this theme.

The tools in this section are essentially solo therapy; they're self-life-coaching sessions that ask you revealing questions about your past, your present, and what you want for your future—where you are, how you got there, and the direction you're heading—and reveal to you the blocks limiting you from achieving your dreams.

A therapist listens and asks the right questions, allowing someone to dive deeper and deeper and peel away the layers of what they're feeling, and journaling afforded me the same process: to get to the core of my issue; understand where it came from and how long it had been there; and gain perspective and clarity on what my real beliefs were, why I was covering them up, and with what. In my case, a core belief of not being good enough manifested in believing *my body* was not good enough, which led to my eating disorder.

While I love and believe strongly in the benefits of traditional therapy—and if you are struggling with any life-threatening issues, please seek out professional help *immediately*—the tools in this section are powerful in their own right because the absence of another person allows for more authenticity straightaway, since there's no fear of judgment from the paper. While it may take time with a therapist to build the high level of trust needed to divulge deep insights from your past and admit your dark thoughts and beliefs, when you're doing this work on your own or in conjunction with therapy, it becomes easier to go there with yourself right off the bat. There's comfort knowing no one has to read your words—ever. You can be as dark and deep as you need to in order to get to the core of what needs to be revealed.

I'm happy to report I've learned to love myself at my natural weight instead of relapsing into anorexia. That's just one of the wonders of journaling. So whatever your most pressing issue or limiting belief, allow journaling to become a major tool in your arsenal for letting it out.

So go slow, savor, and enjoy the power of these revealing techniques.

- 49 The "Of Course" Tool
- 50 The Worst-Case-Scenario Breakdown
- 51 The Hunt-for-Light-in-the-Dark Tool
- 52 The Limit Buster
- 53 The Confusion Clearer
- 54 The Chat with God
- 55 The Create-Your-Own Tool

THE "OF COURSE" TOOL

Steve Jobs famously said, "You can't connect the dots looking forward; you can only connect them looking backward." This quote comes up on almost every podcast interview I record with fascinating people because when they start telling their stories, it's obvious how divine every step was, leading them to where they are now. However, when they were in the thick of it, they had no idea where their current situation could lead.

For instance, my mentor Gabby Bernstein was an entrepreneur at the age of 21, owning a PR company promoting nightclubs, and now she's a world-famous self-help author and inspirational speaker. While Gabby didn't know this at the time, her experience as both an entrepreneur and a publicist gave her the skills she needed to promote her work now so it can reach and help millions of people—something she might have struggled with if she hadn't had this previous life experience. Now, in addition to being one of the most sought-after spiritual teachers of our time, she's a powerful marketer and businesswoman whose work has been featured around the globe. While her work itself is noteworthy, her background in PR was instrumental in helping her spread her message by landing media coverage everywhere from The New York Times to Oprah. She now even blends both passions, spirituality and business, to train other up-and-coming spiritual teachers in her master class. Clearly, everything happens for a reason, even if you have no clue what that reason is yet.

This tool is an opportunity for you to look back on the events in your life and see why—of course—they happened the way they did, and how even events that seemed negative or mundane in the moment were necessary in the course of your life journey. We often say things happen *to us,* but what if life actually happens *through us?* This tool allows you to connect the dots in the past to see clearly how powerful you are in creating your future.

Directions:

- *Step 1:* Choose both a recent positive situation and a recent negative situation from the past year. Write these out and then add the words "of course" at the end of each sentence.

  For instance, a positive situation would look like, *"I found the perfect place to live, of course."* A negative one would look like, *"I lost my job, of course."*

- *Step 2:* Underneath each sentence, list all the ways in which you can see how, looking back, you played a part in creating that reality.

  For instance:

I found the perfect place to live, of course, because I've been open to new places I wouldn't normally live, I'm been remaining calm and trusting I'll find the best place without searching frantically, I've been proactive about asking people who need roommates, yet I've remained unattached to the outcome . . .

I lost my job, of course, because it's not what I actually want to be doing anyway, I always had a bad attitude, I desire a new job, it was a distraction for me to not live my dream, and I never gave it my all . . .

THE WORST-CASE-SCENARIO BREAKDOWN

Inspiration for the tools in this book came from literally everywhere. I mostly crafted them based on what I needed journaling prompts for or what my clients and friends were dealing with—but this one was created *before* there was a need for it. It was inspired by the lyrics of a song I heard while writing. I was instantly moved to create a tool based on the refrain of the Jaymay song "Never Be Daunted." (That's the cool thing about inspiration—it can hit you anytime, anywhere.)

To me, this song depicts the common dilemma many of us find ourselves in of fearing a future outcome that is not only *not here yet,* but also likely *may never come.* I asked myself, *Why do we waste our energy thinking about those outcomes?* If we spend our lives obsessing and worrying about worst-case scenarios, not only are we essentially praying them into existence (since as you know by now, I believe that what we focus on becomes our reality), but more important we're not allowing ourselves to be happy in the moment that we're currently in.

This tool guides you to reveal and release your worst-case-scenario thoughts so you can relish the reality that is and not worry about a future outcome that hasn't happened yet or likely will never happen. Whether you're enduring the stress of final exams *(What if I fail out, never find my dream job, and have to live with my parents for 10 more years?)*, the excitement of a new relationship, or the emotions of ending one *(What if I never find my soul mate and end up alone for the rest of my life?)*, pull back from future thoughts and just be in the moment. As author Nancy Levin says in one of my favorite quotes ever: "Relish the space between no longer and not yet."

Directions:

- *Step 1:* Set a timer for one minute.

- *Step 2:* You have exactly one minute and not a second longer to let out all your fearful and negative thoughts and worries about worst-case scenarios that have been running your mind. When the timer goes off *you have to stop*—this is key. (Remember, the more you focus on the negative, the more it might happen. Um, do you want that? No. So follow this direction!) Go!

- *Step 3:* Now tear that page out of your journal. Rip it up into little pieces. Scatter them in the toilet.

- *Step 4: Optional and a bit graphic.* Go to the bathroom in said toilet and then flush. Take a sigh of relief as all your worries are flushed away.

- *Step 5:* Get present. Close this book. Get out of the house. Go outside. Do something fun. Enjoy yourself. Relish the moment without fear of the future because *it's not happening now and may never happen.* And remember, you flushed all that shit down the toilet anyway.

THE HUNT-FOR-LIGHT-IN-THE-DARK TOOL

When I began to gain weight over time after my eating disorder, at first I felt okay about it. I knew I needed to put on weight for my health, and during this in-between time, my body was still ultra-thin, but slightly less thin than it was at my lowest, so people were no longer concerned. I was eating whatever I desired, legalizing foods that had been off-limits for years, not being obsessive about exercise, and finding pleasure in food again.

Then one day, a couple of years into that process, I woke up and realized I had gained more weight than I was comfortable with. While that might seem like a good thing, to me it was terrifying. Although it was gradual, it hit me hard in one day. My body wasn't "special" anymore: It wasn't something that needed healing or attention any longer, but was average—which made *me* feel average, not special, and therefore not good enough to shine. My worth as a human was so utterly wrapped up in my weight and physical body that I felt like a failure.

I had to make a choice. Option 1 was to go back to my old ways of restrictive, life-consuming dieting and try to get my body back to where it was when I felt comfortable and confident. Or Option 2: I could try to gain that comfort and confidence in the body I was in. I knew the path to Option 1; I had done it before and could probably do it again—but did I want to? Option 2 was saner but unknown, and perhaps impossible. I felt stuck.

Every day I was consumed by this dilemma, and I didn't understand how it was possible for me to be confident in my body regardless of my size. If my life ended here, then perhaps I wouldn't have to try either option. As crazy as it sounds, that's what I wished for months. I spent a lot of time alone, not wanting to get out of bed in the morning.

Many people can likely relate to such a deep, dark depression. While weight and body image might not be your catalyst like they were for me, there are many factors that can catapult you mentally to a place where getting out of bed to face another day is the last thing you want to do. The hardest part for me was that most people didn't know what I was going through. During the phase of my eating disorder where I was severely underweight, I wore the disease visibly for all to see; but with *this* phase where the self-hatred thoughts were even deeper—no one was concerned or even looking at me. I looked fine, healthy even, but mentally I was silently, severely struggling.

During this time I turned to my journal more than ever before. I sought professional help, too, but my journal was somewhere I could let out all the dark, terrible thoughts I was having all the time on a moment-to-moment basis—and when I could see them written out in front of me, I could look at them objectively. This exercise is how I got myself out of bed during that dark time, and I credit it with bringing light back into my life after many months of mental blackout.

Directions:

- *Step 1:* **Release the self-hate.** First, write down your deep emotions and thoughts in real time, even if they seem too dark to admit to another person. Carry around a journal in your bag so that you always have an outlet, and write in your phone if your journal isn't available or you'd feel too conspicuous using it. In my experience, it's best to write each morning, even when you don't want to, as well as anytime you feel overcome with emotion. That is what I did every day.

- *Step 2:* **Have a conversation with yourself.** Next, have a conversation with yourself on the page. Ask yourself probing questions, trying to get any positive response you can. When I did this, I kind of felt like a clown trying to make a scared child laugh—doing all I could. Here are some questions to get you started: *What if these feelings could all release? Wouldn't it be nice if I felt zest for life again? How would that feel? Is that possible for me? How? What if my life could be better? How would that feel? How would I feel? How would I act?*

  It may be hard to find answers to these questions—it was for me most days—but I encourage you to try. Sometimes hitting the right questions will allow answers you didn't know were within you to come out. They can surprise you by comforting you in the exact way you need to hear.

- *Step 3:* **Repeat.** Repeat this exercise every day, letting out the dark and searching deep within you like a treasure hunt for any light that is in there. Where there is light, there can't be dark. Over time you'll be able to pull more and more light out of you, illuminating your reasons to live and slowly diminishing the darkness clouding your life.

THE LIMIT BUSTER

Have you ever thought, *really* thought, about what it is you most want? If so, have you allowed yourself to go after it . . . or are you held back by limitations? This tool, used consistently, will help you bust through all the ways you may be limiting yourself from reaching your full potential and living a limitlessly joyful existence.

I love this tool because it's essentially a small collage of deep questions that get into all the dark corners of your mind, asking you things you might not have allowed yourself to even think about. Just like when you meet someone new and ask them questions to get an idea of who they are and what they enjoy, this tool does the same with getting to know *you*—only your true self, your soul. Its questions reveal to you not only a little more about what's pleasurable to you, but how you can bust through your perceived limitations to create more of what you want in your life. So be introspective, and dive into each of the questions. Be deeply honest with yourself.

Directions:

- *Step 1:* Freewrite on these questions: Where do you feel deprived in your life, and what do you want more of? What is lacking in your current situation?

- *Step 2:* Complete this sentence:

  If I knew I wouldn't disappoint anyone or fail, I would_____.

  Write about how that would feel.

- *Step 3:* What's stopping you?

- *Step 4:* What is *one* positive routine you could put into place for 30 days in the direction of what you wrote about above? What would committing to this for 30 days feel like?

- *Step 5:* Now, what are some things that you could *take off* your plate to create space? For instance, identify some things you do out of habit that aren't things you actually enjoy or have no positive return on investment in your life. How would clearing this space make you feel?

- *Step 6:* Complete the sentence:

  It will be amazing when I_____.

THE CONFUSION CLEARER

I believe few feelings feel worse than confusion. With sadness, you at least know you're sad; with anger, you know you're angry—you can *feel* those emotions and take steps to move through them. But with confusion, you might not even realize the emotion you need to feel, so you're paralyzed, stuck, unable to move forward.

Shifting your energy through writing is powerful and will help you find what it is you need to feel. Have you ever found clarity by talking something out with a trusted friend or mentor who's been there and can relate? That's what this tool does for you, but in a more creative way. You're writing a letter not only to someone who's been through a similar situation and made it out alive, but better yet someone who's been through an *identical* situation—your future self.

Your future self will help guide you through the confusion, gain a new perspective, and move forward. By allowing yourself to first rant, you'll naturally begin to want to self-soothe. You might even see that it's actually not as bad as you first thought, now knowing there's a way out, and start to search for gratitude within it.

Now this may be a bit esoteric, but I believe time might not be linear, and the past and present and future all exist at once on different planes . . . and if that's true—why can't we speak to our future self and ask them for some guidance? They're out there in time and space existing simultaneously *somewhere,* aren't they? And even if they're not, whatever. This tool is still massively helpful.

Directions:

- *Step 1:* **Dear Future Self . . .** Begin writing a letter. Address the letter to your future self—who is already out of the confusion you're in right now. Start the letter with all that's on your mind. Vent about how you're feeling in the moment and what you're stuck or confused about, being as honest and direct as you need to be. Vocalize all your worries, fears, and doubts. Don't hold anything back. As you write, notice what feelings come up. Are you ranting and angry? Are you feeling more sorrowful? Go ahead and vent; your future self won't mind. Her life is so awesome that she can handle it.

- *Step 2:* **Dear Current Self . . .** Once every bit of how you're feeling has come out of you, begin to pivot to the positive. From there, write a response *as* your future self. Remind your current self all that *is* working—all you have to be grateful for, all you have to be excited about. Remember, your future self has already been through your current situation and come out on the other side. No one knows what would be most healing to hear better than she does. Can she offer any advice about your current situation? What does it look like from her perspective?

Forcing yourself to focus on the positive will remind you of what you love about your life. So whatever is stressing you out and confusing you in the moment—be it your relationship, your job or career, your finances, anything—this will ground you back to the good within it and leave you with a sense that you will come out on the other side stronger and wiser. Remember, this letter is just for you, so don't edit for spelling or grammar; simply allow your thoughts to flow onto the page.

THE CHAT WITH GOD

Your relationship with God (insert higher-power word of choice) is just like any other relationship, in that it builds over time. The more you ask for guidance, the more you are given; the more clarity you have for what you want, the more guidance you will hear for what you desire. Think of this tool as a friendship builder, only it's helping you build a relationship with God.

To me, *God* is a word that describes our infinite capacity for love, beauty, and support. It's that piece inside of us all that is the same . . . that we all came into the world with as babies. God is our intuition, our soul, our inspired creativity; and to me God is the Universe, Source, Mother Nature, and Love. Anytime you feel bliss, relief, or pure joy—that's God. Maybe you've felt that bliss in fleeting moments looking at a newborn, in a yoga class, at the beach, having sex, or on a run. It's the force I often marvel at when I'm at a concert watching an inspired live performance or watching the leaves turn vivid reds in the fall, die in the winter, and bud every spring without fail right around my birthday.

There are lots of ways to connect with God. I feel God's presence when I experience synchronicities: the parking space opening right in front, the rain letting up the second I go outside, the phone ringing as I'm thinking of a friend.

These things make me feel supported, connected, cared for, and guided, which to me is pure love and support—how I define God.

What is God to you? How do you speak with that soul-self inside you that's been within you since you were the size of a loaf of bread?

This tool is a guide to getting started speaking and listening to God in a new way. It's a sacred practice and can be done often. While many people communicate with God through prayer or meditation, this tool is a written form of both. Through prayer, we are speaking to God; through meditation, we are listening and soaking up guidance. Try to give yourself some space for it, though, perhaps by being alone and in a comfortable space. When you're in a relaxed, calm state, you can hear more guidance coming to you. And when you're at peace, you can allow more peace to come through you and become you again, because peace is your true nature—anything other than peace is simply stuff you picked up from your environment and circumstances.

Use this tool whenever you need to feel comfort, restore your peace, and gain guidance.

Directions:

Note: For this exercise you will need two colors of pens.

- *Step 1:* **Journaling prayer . . . speaking to God.** Begin with one color pen. Let out all your feelings, insecurities, or things you'd be willing to surrender to a power that is greater than you. Write down everything you're willing to let go of and ask for help with. These things can be big or small. You can ask questions or simply make statements about how you're feeling in the moment. By letting these things out and surrendering them to God/Source/Universe, you're letting go and allowing a force (that can, as Marianne Williamson often says, turn an acorn into an oak tree, or an embryo into a baby) to take the wheel instead of you.

- *Step 2:* **Journaling meditation . . . listening to God.** Now exhale deeply and sit in a minute of stillness meditation, just listening and soaking up guidance. Then grab your other color pen and begin to freewrite for at least five minutes, allowing the words to just pass through you. Try not to judge them or even read them as you write them down—just allow them to move through you. This advice can be simple or complex; just trust that whatever wants to come through is the guidance you are asking for.

- *Step 3:* Read over the guidance you received and, in the first color pen, underline those nuggets of wisdom or gems from the freewriting that you will follow up on or allow to guide you. Perhaps take some of that wisdom and put it on note cards or sticky notes so that you can keep the messages with you. I do this all the time and keep these messages from God/my higher self with me everywhere, from the background of my phone to the dashboard of my car.

THE CREATE-YOUR-OWN TOOL

(The Last Tool)

No matter how many self-help books you've read (or protocols you've followed, or techniques you've tried), you may still feel the information doesn't fully integrate into your life like it did for the author, even if you follow their steps perfectly. For me, when an exercise routine, business technique, recipe, or self-help strategy didn't produce the same results in my life as it did for the creator, I used to immediately think I must not have done something right or long enough or well enough—but then I realized, what if the flaw wasn't with me? What if the flaw was with the program?

Sometimes even the most helpful information doesn't work for us because it is based on the author's or creator's needs and wants, and isn't fully tailored to our own. While it's wonderful to share experiences, it's impossible to know exactly to a T what works for everyone because the secret is: nothing works for everyone. (Thankfully. If we were all cookie-cutter identical clones, how boring would life be?)

And while it's rad to hear other authors' inspiring stories, success plans, diet regimens, and healing protocols, remember that it's just that—*inspiration*—and ultimately only *you* have the self-awareness to know what will work best in your life. I saw this time and again with myself with diet books. I'd think, *Okay, I'll just do exactly what she did, and then I'll be happy*—but that was never the case, because while there was great wisdom in what the author shared, ultimately it was the plan that worked for them; they can't possibly know whether it would work for everyone the same way. Of course it's awesome to have coaches and mentors to inspire you, notice your blind spots, and motivate you to stay on track to your desires, but follow nothing as fact *except* what your intuition tells you.

Therefore, this tool puts you in the driver's seat. You'll make your own questions here, because you know the areas you need to examine better than I (or anyone) ever could. This tool allows you to get into not only those deep areas you need to explore but also those fun questions that you might never really allow yourself to daydream about.

All the other tools in this book will be here for whenever you need a journaling tune-up or guidance, but right now you have full creative license to take the reins and choose your own words, which is actually best because you intuitively know how best to inspire yourself more than I do. Now that you've been on a journey of letting it out with me as your guide, it's your turn to take the wheel on the practice of journaling and use your newfound self-awareness to find the questions you need most to answer.

Directions:

- *Step 1:* **Create.** Pick one category from below, and then write three to five go-to questions to ask yourself when you're in these situations:

  - *Category 1:* You find yourself in a negative energy and need to write your way out.

  - *Category 2:* You find yourself confused and need to figure out what you're feeling.

  - *Category 3:* You feel awesome and simply want to stay in that space—and figure out how you manifested such an awesome state.

  Be sure the questions you create on the category you choose are authentic to you and lead you where you most need to explore. Make sure you love them enough to always feel inspired to write on *at least* one of them when you need a probing writing prompt.

  Here are a few questions I use if you need inspiration:

- *How could I be more loving to myself today?*

- *What am I grateful for in this exact moment?*

- *What is a positive outcome I could dream about?*

- *How could I surprise, help, or flirt with someone today?*

- *What am I most excited about right now?*

- *How will I be more awesome as a result of the challenge I'm in the midst of right now?*

- *Step 2:* **Use.** Keep the questions you created in Step 1 somewhere handy (the Notes app in your iPhone is a rad spot). If you wrote questions in response to one of the first two categories, become aware when any negative thought patterns or old beliefs creep into your mind—recognize that they are unproductive to dwell on, and decide to do something about it. The remedy of choice here: journaling (duh). Your questions will help you shift out of negativity and find clarity by feeling your emotions fully, the more you move down the page.

  However, there's no need to use this tool exclusively for negative or confusing moments. Rather than being an SOS journaler, I recommend that you journal when your life is *fantastic* just as much as when it feels like it's falling apart. The more you journal when things are awesome, the more you'll feel the richness of that bliss. Plus, it allows you to realize how you got into this high-vibe state and, most important, how to *stay there* and *return to* that level of awesome if you wander out.

AFTERWORD

"The knowledge of the past stays with us. To let go is to release the images and emotions, the grudges and fears, the clingings and disappointments of the past that bind our spirit."
— JACK KORNFIELD

I feel so proud that I've been able to collage together what has healed me, revealed so much to me, organized my life, and gotten me going on the path to living my dreams into what is now a method for you to begin the practice of *letting it out.* As I finish this book, I find myself launching into worry mode—not because I poured my heart and soul into every tool, but because I'm so positive these tools have the power to transform lives that the thought of not getting this book into the hands of everyone it could help makes me feel deep obligation and extreme duty with a big side of nervousness. Clearly, this is something I need to use my tools for, so that I can release my attachment and trust this book will reach everyone who needs its message. It is my responsibility to just let go and allow.

I believe everything happens for a reason, and we're all playing a role in a perfect divine plan, where at any given time you're both the star of your own story and an extra in someone else's. Chances are my book got into your hands for a reason. Maybe it caught your eye on the shelf or was given to you as a gift, or you stumbled across my website. Either way, you were led to this journey for a reason, and I believe that if you didn't need this message, you wouldn't be holding this book in your hands. These tools were made for you. I wrote them for me based on what I needed, but I believe we're really all one, so therefore I wrote them for you based on what you might need, too.

Perhaps on first read some of these tools seemed too esoteric or deep, and you preferred to stick to the lighter ones. That's fine; the heavy lifting of this book is not required all at once; however, it *is* required eventually. Deeply feeling your emotions is your only way to truly move through them. While there are many ways to do this, writing is an extremely powerful one, and I believe that your reading this book is a sign that you're like me—writing is your way through to all you need to feel, reveal, and heal in your life. Like I've said a million times, I'm not aware of how I'm feeling unless I'm writing. If you're reading this, whether you realize it or not, chances are this is likely the case for you, too. Perhaps it's not the time for you now, but in a few months you just might return to it, dust it off from your bookshelf, and say, "Oh, *now* I see what that girl was saying, and I'm ready to feel my feelings through writing." This book will be there for you as your guide.

If you use these tools repeatedly, consistently, and honestly, it's impossible for them not to work for you. And if you're not sure whether they're working, here's test: Do you feel good when you're writing? Do you feel relief when you've gotten radically honest on the page? If you do, then they're working. That feeling of relief is literally the Universe patting you on the back, saying, "You've got this. Keep going."

If I hadn't been writing in my journal, I wouldn't have heard the precious guidance and lessons or created change in my life to call in all I dreamed of and more. Obviously, the impact journaling has had and continues to have on my life has been tremendous, and I still practice these methods daily and feel "off" if I miss a day or two. I hope journaling becomes a significant practice in your life as it has in mine. I believe in these tools so strongly, and I am humbled and grateful you've allowed me to lead you on this journey to *Let It Out.*

Keep it handy, keep in touch, and keep writing. *Namaste.*

KATIE'S
RECOURSE GUIDE

I've been on the path of spirituality and self-development for a while now, and getting to where I am was not something I did alone. I've had many mentors who have inspired and helped me along the way. If you're sparked with inspiration to continue your growth and take your expansion outside the pages of this book, here are some resources I suggest. Curating high-vibe content is one of my most favorite things to do, and the below is just the tip of the iceberg. If you want more, please visit my website: www.katiedalebout.com.

Gabrielle Bernstein: Gabby got me started on this path. After reading her first book, my entire life and perspective shifted. It was a true miracle and gift. Since then I've become a connoisseur of her work and have participated in basically everything she creates. Check her out at www.Gabbyb.tv.

Isabel Foxen Duke: Isabel is a radical teacher who changed the way I feel about food and my body. I owe so much to her and her teaching and could not recommend her online course Stop Fighting Food more. Her unique perspective on weight and body image changed my life and shifted everything in me, and it has the power to shift society and make us all happier. www.isabelfoxenduke.com

Mastin Kipp: Mastin is a fiercely authentic and modern spiritual teacher. His work is something I deeply connect to, and I'd recommend anything he produces. www.thedailylove.com

Marie Forleo: Marie is the founder of B-School, an online program to learn how to make money and a difference online. She has many free resources online as well, and I would also recommend anything she creates. www.marieforleo.com

Alex Beadon: Alex is an amazing leader when it comes to helping online entrepreneurs turn their passion into their profession. Her technical skills combined with her patience and passion make her the ideal teacher for breaking down the sometimes-scary technical side of online business creation; her online products and courses are user-friendly and simple to use. www.alexbeadon.com

Elle Griffin: Elle is the editor-in-chief of *Over the Moon* magazine, on online journal where the Divine Feminine comes to party. Her guidance and wisdom have made this book possible and helped me achieve every success in my life, including connecting to my Divine Feminine power and potential. www.overthemoonmag.com

Elizabeth Gilbert: Ms. Gilbert is my writing hero, and I so highly recommend everything she writes and creates. She's a fierce woman changing the landscape for literary women. Her newest book, *Big Magic,* is a must-read for all creative people. www.elizabethgilbert.com

Danielle LaPorte: Danielle is another powerhouse woman who's up to massively big things and helping women create what she calls "goals with soul" through her immensely powerful book and movement *The Desire Map.* Her work inspires me tremendously. www.daniellelaporte.com

Kate Northrup: If financial freedom is what you're after, Kate, author of *Money: A Love Story,* is your girl. She's the queen of helping people achieve financial freedom. www .katenorthrup.com

Jessica Ortner: Jessica is basically the princess of tapping or Emotional Freedom Technique (EFT), which is an incredibly powerful technique that uses ancient acupressure points to relieve everything from chronic pain to trauma to stress. She's massively knowledgeable about body image and weight struggles, since she herself has struggled in those areas and healed with the help of EFT. www.jessicaortner.com

Kris Carr: When it comes to healing holistically, Kris is the queen. She was diagnosed with cancer young, which led her to embark on a Crazy Sexy healing journey through food, a lot of green juice, self-love, and wellness practices that she outlines in her books and products. www.kriscarr.com

Tara Stiles: When it comes to yoga, Tara Stiles is the reigning princess—however, there's so much more to this woman than doing splits and being able to top up into a handstand everywhere from airports to yoga studios. She's created an entire movement around her mantra of "make your own rules" and is one of the humblest teachers I've ever met. Having struggled with eating disorders herself in her past, she's like a big sister to me. She's written on everything from yoga to mindfulness to food. She is awesome. www.tarastiles.com

Hay House: My publisher, Hay House—founded by trailblazer Louise Hay, the leader of the new thought movement—has been instrumental in my personal growth journey. Each year they host the Hay House World Summit where they feature over 100 self-help teachers, authors, and speakers. These summits introduce me to new ideas and people from all over the world with unique perspectives on health, wellness, and spirituality every year. I have personally participated in many live workshops and events they offer, and could not speak more highly of my experience. www .hayhouse.com

The Wellness Wonderland Method: If you're looking to deepen your journaling practice and take your life to the next level, my mentorship program offers exclusive one-on-one coaching, including biweekly calls and personalized exercises, resources, and inspiration. I also offer group coaching and have built a powerful community to inspire radical authenticity in an inclusive, safe place to share our experience. Find out more at my website: www.katiedalebout.com.

For more of my recommended resources, including everything from my favorite inspiring books, movies, quotes, foods, videos, and more, visit www.katiedalebout.com/starthere to get my complimentary Quick Start Guide to Living in Wellness Wonderland with links to literally everything I love. This guide is constantly updated since I'm always finding cool things to share.

If you want more inspiration from me on a weekly basis, and to hear what my voice sounds like, subscribe to my podcast, *The Wellness Wonderland Radio*, on iTunes. I've interviewed many of the people I mention throughout this book.

ACKNOWLEDGMENTS

This book is a collage inspired by the many spiritual and personal-development teachers who have tremendously impacted me on my journey. This book is an interpretation of the wisdom I gained from your teachings, and it is dedicated to you.

To my teacher Gabrielle Bernstein, you showed me what was possible with openness, desire, and hustle. Thank you for being my guide, mentor, and friend, and showing me that the spark I saw in you as a lost college student was a reflection of a light within me as a determined young woman.

To Isabel Foxen Duke, you are a trailblazer in your field, and your dedication to your message is massively inspiring to me. I'm so grateful for you and your dedication to changing society's misconceptions. I wish I could implant your message into the mind of every woman who needs it.

I'd like to thank all my podcast guests for sharing their truth with me one-on-one on my show, including Kate Northrup, Robyn Youkilis, Quinn Asteak, Latham Thomas, Christy Harrison, Jessica Ortner, Tara Stiles, Nancy Levin, and so many more beautiful teachers and authors who gave their time to mentor me.

To the memory of Jess Ainscough, aka the Wellness Warrior, you inspired me so much in your short life—to start my blog and even to enter the writing contest with our publisher,

Hay House, that led to this book. Thank you for your beautiful spirit; your memory will live on forever.

To the loving Hay House family, Louise Hay, Reid Tracy, Nancy Levin, Patty Gift, and Sally Mason, for being so nice and welcoming to me and giving young first-time authors like myself a chance to share our light with the world by hosting your annual Writers Workshops. You made my dream a reality.

Most of all to my editor, Lindsay DiGianvittorio, for your patience, your guidance, and encouragement through the writing process—you are the reason this book is good. Your suggestions, compliments, and edits made this book something I'm really proud of, and I'm so grateful for you. I couldn't have asked for a better, more skilled partner to help me with this project.

Special thanks to my best friend and photographer Abbey Moore for capturing the joy that the practice of journaling gives me. To my best friend Laura Evangelista for doing (many drafts of) the beautiful cover design to get this book into the hands of all those who do judge a book by its cover. And to my copyeditor Esmé Wang, thanks for all your help early on.

To Adam Rossi, for holding my hand through writing the book proposal and so many other things—this book and a lot of other things would not exist without you; you are so awesome. To my first boss, Jessica Spires, you taught me how to conduct myself in the world with grace. I'm so grateful you believed in my dreams as much as I did; I will never forget your kindness.

To Dana Brown and Katy Wright—I love you guys. To Ellen Connor and Maria Castaneda for being and making me cool—I'm never stepping out of our BOX. To my friend Carly

Morgan Gross, thanks for being my sounding board and for being so real with me since the first time we spoke; your fearlessness inspires me. To Erin Haslag, for always being there to help me with everything from breakups to website breakdowns; you are my big sister, mentor, and friend that I manifested thanks to Hay House. Thank you to Heather Waxman for collaborating with me and singing the *Let It Out* theme song; you are an angel and I'm in awe of your talents. To Stephanie Kirylych for being my spiritual running buddy and humble, beautiful friend. To Sacha Jones, you are my non-birth mama, healer, and friend who was so supportive to me from day one of this book's inception. To Simi Botic for being my friend and such a positive role model in every area of life.

To my coaches: Filippa Salomonsson for opening my eyes to this Hay House world; Elle Griffin for taking me over the moon with my life, expression, health, projects, and faith; and Cora Poage for seeing my blind spots and teaching me presence and how to live a limitless life. You three are the big sisters I always dreamed of, and I'm so grateful for you all.

Big gratitude and love to my clients and friends of my blog—you are the girls who showed me these tools work not only for me but for all humans who are open to change. Thank you for being my guinea pigs for these tools and citizens of my Wellness Wonderland—I adore you all.

Finally to my mom, for ingraining in me that anything is possible, accompanying me on my pilgrimage to Manhattan to meet my gurus and participate in the contest that would lead to this book, and being my biggest fan and doing everything so I would have a great life. To my dad, for always helping me move, being a genuinely nice guy, and for making me watch *Seinfeld* with you as a young child.

To my aunts, uncles, cousins, and grandparents for listening to me preach, holding space for me as I typed my way through this book, and being open to me as I passionately, and very vocally, shared my experience with self-help and spirituality. I love you *all* more than you know. Thank you for raising me. It wasn't just my parents; it was you guys—you know who you are. Thanks for being my village.

Peace, love, and words.

ABOUT THE AUTHOR

Through her writing, podcasts, videos, and courses, millennial blogger, speaker, and podcast host **Katie Dalebout** curates inspired wisdom that guides people to go deep and sift through the thoughts clouding their minds. She's a regular contributor to Refinery29 and MindBodyGreen, and her work has been featured in *Teen Vogue*, Yahoo! Health, and *The Daily Mail*. In 2013 Katie launched the weekly interview podcast *WWRadio*, which attracted wellness and lifestyle celebrities such as Gabrielle Bernstein, Tara Stiles, and Joe Cross in its first few episodes. Katie helps people develop a positive image of their bodies through embracing their creativity and personality outside of their physicality, and she's on a mission to share journaling tools that invoke deeper authenticity and true self-acceptance. If you'd like more inspiration from Katie, visit her in Wellness Wonderland at www.katiedalebout.com or follow her on Instagram, Facebook, Twitter, and YouTube: @katiedalebout.

Hay House Titles of Related Interest

YOU CAN HEAL YOUR LIFE, the movie,
starring Louise Hay & Friends
(available as a 1-DVD program and an expanded 2-DVD set)
Watch the trailer at: www.LouiseHayMovie.com

THE SHIFT, the movie,
starring Dr. Wayne W. Dyer
(available as a 1-DVD program and an expanded 2-DVD set)
Watch the trailer at: www.DyerMovie.com

Daily Love: Growing into Grace, by Mastin Kipp

*Light Is the New Black: A Guide to Answering Your Soul's
Callings and Working Your Light,* by Rebecca Campbell

Make Your Own Rules Diet, by Tara Stiles

*Miracles Now: 108 Life-Changing Tools for Less Stress, More
Flow, and Finding Your True Purpose,* by Gabrielle Bernstein

Reveal: A Sacred Manual for Getting Spiritually Naked,
by Meggan Watterson

*Shadows Before Dawn: Finding the Light of Self-Love
Through Your Darkest Times,* by Teal Swan

We hope you enjoyed this Hay House book. If you'd like to receive our online catalog featuring additional information on Hay House books and products, or if you'd like to find out more about the Hay Foundation, please contact:

Hay House, Inc., P.O. Box 5100, Carlsbad, CA 92018-5100
(760) 431-7695 or (800) 654-5126
(760) 431-6948 (fax) or (800) 650-5115 (fax)
www.hayhouse.com® • www.hayfoundation.org

Published and distributed in Australia by:
Hay House Australia Pty. Ltd., 18/36 Ralph St., Alexandria NSW 2015
Phone: 612-9669-4299 • *Fax:* 612-9669-4144 • www.hayhouse.com.au

Published and distributed in the United Kingdom by:
Hay House UK, Ltd., Astley House, 33 Notting Hill Gate, London W11 3JQ
Phone: 44-20-3675-2450 • *Fax:* 44-20-3675-2451 • www.hayhouse.co.uk

Published and distributed in the Republic of South Africa by:
Hay House SA (Pty), Ltd., P.O. Box 990, Witkoppen 2068
info@hayhouse.co.za • www.hayhouse.co.za

Published in India by: Hay House Publishers India,
Muskaan Complex, Plot No. 3, B-2, Vasant Kunj, New Delhi 110 070
Phone: 91-11-4176-1620 • *Fax:* 91-11-4176-1630 • www.hayhouse.co.in

Distributed in Canada by: Raincoast Books,
440 Viking Way, Richmond, B.C. V6V 1N2
Phone: 1-800-663-5714 • *Fax:* 1-800-565-3770 • www.raincoast.com

Take Your Soul on a Vacation

Visit www.HealYourLife.com® to regroup,
recharge, and reconnect with your own magnificence.
Featuring blogs, mind-body-spirit news, and
life-changing wisdom from Louise Hay and friends.

Visit www.HealYourLife.com today!